CA

Dr Carson I. A. Ritchie, author of many craft books and articles, is also an ivory carver and Associate Member of the Royal Society of Miniature Artists. He has had a shared exhibition of his work at the Christian Art Centre, All Hallows, London Wall, London, and a one-man exhibition at Foyle's Art Gallery, London. Every summer he makes a trip to Central Africa, and has learned much by talking to and watching folk artists there. He has lectured in the United States, as Visiting Professor at Notre Dame University, and besides his craft and history of art books he has edited a number of texts and written several historical books.

Dr Ritchie is the author of *Papercraft*, available in this series.

TEACH YOURSELF BOOKS

CANDLEMAKING

Carson Ritchie

TEACH YOURSELF BOOKS
Hodder and Stoughton

First printed 1976

ISBN 0 340 20389 7
Printed and bound in Great Britain for Teach Yourself Books, Hodder and Stoughton, London, by Fletcher & Son Ltd, Norwich

Contents

Preface

Why should people want to make candles? One of the reasons is very simple—people like candles. A flame is a constant companion, a sort of inanimate pet, which responds to our actions. When we move about, it moves too, influenced by the currents of air we create. Not merely does the candle respond to us, we respond to it. Candles are all that are left of our ancestral hearth fires, the last flickers of our old friend, flame, which has been with us since the Stone Age. As someone who has set three chimneys on fire, I am not going to deplore unduly the passing of the open fire. Yet fires, like smoking, or burning incense, appeal to some strongly developed but unvoiced instinct in man. Anyone who has ever observed a child looking at a candle will be aware of this instinct, even though he may not be able to define it. Man needs to look at a naked flame from time to time, just as he does green fields, and it may be that the former will create a greater awareness and stimulate him more even than the latter.

> 'Down through the ages marches Man, changing yet still the same.
> And he worships still in his heart of hearts, the God of fire and flame.'

There is another very good reason for making candles. Candlemaking is the one art form that has not been overrun by professionalism. There are courses in candlemaking, and you can buy books about it, like this one; but there are no certificates to be taken in it, much less degrees. Yet no one who has looked at as many modern candles as I have would deny that candlemaking is just as much an art form in its own right as any that we have today. Because it is a completely new art form, however (despite its storied past, which we will examine in a moment), everyone who enters it starts equal. You have just as great a chance of becoming renowned—or of making money by selling your candles—as everyone else has. There will be no tendency for hanging committees on exhibitions to look to see whether you have a string of letters after your name. Nor is this one of the many branches of art in which the only good artist is a dead one.

I have mentioned the profitable side of candlemaking not because I feel an artist ought to be motivated principally by financial gain but because it is often very useful nowadays to make one's amusements gainful ones. If you can persuade yourself, your family and your bank manager that you can turn your hobby to good account, then you can spend time on it without that feeling of guilt which makes many of us neglect hobbies altogether—with the worst possible consequences for ourselves. Not everyone can make a living out of art, but some can make money from anything, including hobbies. Talking to Britain's foremost candlemaker just the other day, I grew indignant that the creations of himself and his associates had never received the attention they merited from the powers that be. 'What public recognition have you ever received?' I asked him. 'Well,' he replied, 'we all have credit cards.'

It is important to recognise that candlemaking does produce a desirable end-product—candles. Even if you cannot sell at a profit all the candles you make, you can always market them to help out your favourite good cause, or simply use them to solve the Christmas and birthday present problem. Everyone likes a candle. So the candlemaker never has the problem of how to dispose of his treasures. At worst he can always burn them himself—no candle is meant to last for ever—and thus make a bright moment in his life.

Carson A. Ritchie
1976

Acknowledgements

The author would like to express his thanks to Stella Mayes Reed, who took the photographs for this book.

I

The History of the Candle

Candles and candlemaking go back to a remote antiquity, so far in fact that already by the time of the book of *Exodus* it seemed unthinkable that the tabernacle should be lit in any way other than by candles. Already, too, these candles were burning in a candlestick of very elaborate and distinctive design, proof of centuries of evolution. 'You shall make a candlestick of pure gold. The base and the shaft of the candlestick shall be made of wrought workmanship, and its sockets, capitals and flowers shall be of uniform design. There shall be six branches going out of the sides of it, three on one side and three on the other, three sockets made like almonds, each with a capital and a flower . . . and on the candlestick itself four sockets made like almonds with their capitals and flowers . . . Its candle snuffers and their trays shall be of pure gold, and the candlestick itself and all its accessories shall be made of a talent of gold.'[1]

The candlestick of the tabernacle can still be seen today on the carvings that ornament the bas reliefs of the Arch of Titus in Rome. It does not hold any candles, however, an indication perhaps that the ancient world was more inclined to lavish ornament on the light holder than on the light itself.

The choice of candles to light the tabernacle emphasises the strong connection that has always existed between candles and the idea of worship. 'The use of artificial lights in religious

[1] *Exodus* xxv. 31 (synopsised).

ceremonies and observances,' wrote A. F. Simpson in the *Dictionary of Religion and Ethics*, 'has been characteristic of religious customs far into antiquity, and is not to be explained by considerations of utility alone. It springs from a sense of the symbolism inherent in nature and in the powers and energies of the visible world. The human mind has a deep presentiment of a world behind and above the senses, and naturally sees in the more striking phenomena of the world the images and symbols of things unseen. Light, the most ethereal of all material things, has long been consecrated as a symbol of Deity, of Godlike qualities and powers, of truth, purity, holiness, of that which enlightens and purifies the soul.'

The use of candles, whether for secular or religious purposes, was not confined to the ancient Hebrews. The Romans developed their own type of candle, originally a thin cord or string smeared with pitch or surrounded by wax. The word 'candle' comes from Latin, though scholars do not appear to be sure whether it derives from *candere*, 'to shine', or from *candelabrum*, the candlestick upon which candles were placed. Besides candles, the Romans used wax torches, often very decorative ones, which can still be seen in tomb paintings and sculptures. Donatus remarks that funerals took their name from the Latin word for these torches, which were lit at funerals and which adorned candelabra set up on these occasions. Pliny tells us that the Romans also used, and apparently invented, rush dips, making from rushes, 'when the bark has been peeled away, candles for lights and for use at funerals'. Originally most Roman candles were made of tallow, a material that offers rather restricted opportunities for ornamentation, but gradually they began to use wax candles as well, first for religious services in the temples (there were several festivals at which candles were regularly burned) and later to light the houses of the great. They constructed massive candlesticks which must have been topped by ornate, impressive and no doubt highly decorated candles, none of which has survived. They used other lights as well, however; Apuleius speaks of 'torches of pinewood, wax candles, tallow candles, and other kinds of light'. Probably because they produced more olive oil than tallow, decoration tended to be concentrated on oil lamps rather than on candles themselves, although ornate candelabra were in regular use. 'When I first came from Asia,' says Trimalchio, a character in a Roman novel, 'I was only as high as this candlestick. But by dint of rubbing candle grease on my chin every night I soon acquired a beard.'

With the passing of ancient times and the arrival of the Dark Ages—ages which were, however, lit by candles—the importance of the candle increases. Western Europe began to be cut off from one of the main sources of olive oil, North Africa, and to rely more on candles for lighting. The religious significance of the candle was also emphasised. Just as the golden candlestick in the tabernacle and the temple was a symbol of the light that shone on the world through law and prophecy, and in the ordinances of religion, so Christ charged His people to be like the candle 'which gives light unto all that are in the house'.

At the end of the Roman Empire, church candles seem regularly to have been made of much more expensive material than ordinary candles for lighting, the latter usually being made from tallow and supplied with a wick of oakum or dried pith of reeds or rushes. Paulinius of Nola (AD 407), describing the feast of St Felix, the patron saint of his church, tells us that 'Lights are burned ordorous with waxed papyri'.

Other religions, such as Islam, also made use of the candle. In medieval Arabic paintings, cherubs can be seen carrying beautifully tapered wax candles. No candles, however, seem to have been as elaborate and decorative as those that were employed in medieval churches. During the Middle Ages candlemaking became a very important branch of Church art. Not only was all the lighting inside the churches provided by candles, but also special candles were produced for the great festivals of the Church. At Easter, for example, a huge candle called the 'Paschal candle', beautifully painted with the figure of a Paschal Lamb, was burned in churches continuously day and night between Holy Saturday and Ascension. At Durham Abbey, now Durham Cathedral, the Paschal candle with its candelabrum stretched from the floor to the vault of the abbey. Other Paschal candles used on the Continent were so tall that they had to be lit from movable pulpits. These candles were the real lighthouses of the faith, fittingly compared by contemporary writers to the pillar of fire which guided the children of Israel in the desert.

We know that the candlemakers of the Middle Ages were consummate artists who could make anything they chose in wax because they often fashioned the wax donated for church candles into a wax statue—usually an image of the donor—which was set up in the church. Several of these images have survived, showing what a robust and long-lasting material wax can be if it receives the right treatment. As the Paschal candles demonstrate, these medieval candlemakers were also capable of producing monster candles, bigger even than those used in antiquity. One Romanesque candelabrum made from marble, now preserved as a treasure in the church of St Paul Without the Walls in Rome, carries a very large candle which is a modern reproduction of the candles that must have burned in it in medieval times.

If it was important to churchmen, the candle played just as large a part in the life of secular folk in the Middle Ages. Candles were the only means of banishing darkness in Britain—

unless, like the Abbot of Aberbrothock, you could be sure of a regular supply of seal oil. It was not always possible to rely on firelight. Monasteries, for instance, only had a fire burning in a special room set aside for the monks to warm themselves. A whole administrative hierarchy developed around the manufacture and supply of candles to the King and his courtiers, and the few others who could afford them. In London two livery companies which are still in existence, the Wax Chandlers and the Tallow Chandlers, were set up to produce candles. Important folk such as the King would be content with nothing but wax. Edward IV's allowance of candles for a winter's day and evening consisted of three torches, one 'tortis' (whatever that was) and three 'prickets', candles with hollow ends which rested on a spike on top of the candlestick. At night he required in his bedchamber six 'perchers', ten wax candles of a size suitable for the room and two wax 'morters' or nightlights.

The real origins of modern candlemaking as a fine art do not appear until the nineteenth century. It was then that craft writers such as the Reverend Godfrey Leland began to instruct their readers in the art of painting church candles, reminding them at the same time that 'the mantelpiece or sideboard at home would gain by suitably ornamented candles being placed on them'. Manufacturers also began to demonstrate the suitability for candles of the newly developed materials stearin and paraffin wax by producing (apparently for the first time) candles moulded into decorative shapes. These shapes were rather simple, such as the 'cable pattern' invented by Messrs Field. The interest in Church art which stemmed from the High Church movement also meant that many English churchgoers now began to see candles regularly in church for the first time since the Reformation. Church candles, incidentally, are still made by hand to a very high standard. Candles used in the Mass by Roman Catholic churches have to be made with at least 65% beeswax, while all other candles used in the church must contain at least 25% beeswax.

Perhaps the most potent feature in awakening an interest in the sculptural beauties of stearin and paraffin wax was nineteenth-century exhibitions, in which pieces of sculpture in these materials began to appear for the first time. The use of these new materials for art work did not always find favour with critics of a more old-fashioned turn of mind. The correspondent of the *Illustrated London News*, visiting the Vienna Exhibition of 1873, quarrelled with the notions of taste that had put on display 'stearin busts of the reigning King and Queen of Holland, and statues of the Venus of Milo, the Diana of the Louvre, and the dancing nymphs of Canova'. 'Another firm in the wax candle line,' he wrote, 'has raised a colossal stearin bust on a lofty pedestal to a certain Milly. The stearin manufactury may be an important branch of German industry, but one does not understand why the Imperial Commissioner of the Vienna Exhibition should have allowed the place to be sown broadcast with competing trophies of it, which are merely so many trade advertisements.'

Whatever art critics thought, ordinary folk seem to have been captivated by the bright clean lines into which the new materials could be cast, and their shining, translucent appearance. They were the first materials that had been developed which would give a cleanly cast candle—tallow had been too soft, beeswax contracts on cooling and so could not be used for casting. It was not surprising that now that materials were available in which really artistic candles could be cast they would sooner or later be developed.

The artistic candle did not appear straight away. The era of the paraffin lamp followed, then electric light. Paradoxically, once the candle disappeared as a normal source of light, its aesthetic possibilities could be rediscovered. And, by an even greater paradox, power strikes have today turned candles back into objects of use as well as of beauty. The twentieth century has seen the acceptance of candles as part of its aesthetic background. Candlelight is discreet. It does not throw over everything that harsh and glaring light which makes objects and people appear at their worst. An age obsessed with personal appearance has discovered the cosmetic qualities of the candle. Candles moisten the often overheated and febrile air in which we live. Their living flame provides a focus and a companionship for our evenings which is just as welcome as it was when man's hands moulded the first candle.

Traditional methods of making candles

A brief survey of candlemaking as an industry rather than an art is essential not merely to understand how the craft developed but also to suggest lines for future experiment by modern candlemakers.

Before the onset of the Industrial Revolution, candlemaking was a home craft. Candles for lighting were formed from byproducts of the kitchen, chiefly tallow obtained usually from beef fat, although mutton suet mixed with ox tallow was also used. Francis Galton, author of *The Art of Travel* (1855), tells us how explorers can procure fat for making candles by breaking marrow bones, boiling them and then skimming off the fat which gathers at the top of the pan. French soldiers in the Crimea were able to make candles in this way when tallow was not available from other sources. Cottagers also made rush lights by stripping the bark from reeds, drying the pith and then dipping the remains of the rush in fat left over from the family meal. In Chapter 14 I have included an extract from the classic account of the whole process of rush-dip making given by the eighteenth-century naturalist Gilbert White of Selborne.

Beeswax candles were always more expensive. They were made by boiling a honeycomb with a little water in a pan for several hours, then pressing the molten mass through a cloth into a deep puddle of cold water. Beeswax is very inflammable, and water was mixed with the comb to prevent it from catching fire. Pure beeswax candles made in this way are still in use in many parts of the world. I have seen old women selling them, along with raw pellets of frankincense, outside the cathedral of St George in Addis Ababa. The candles had thick cotton wicks with fairly thin coatings of wax, proof of the poverty of the faithful who were going to buy them.

From the middle of the eighteenth century, commercial candles, as opposed to home-made ones, began to be turned out by more and more complex machinery. More work was being done at home, after dark, and more candles were needed. Special kinds of craftsmen, such as lacemakers and ivory carvers, tried to get the most out of their candles by burning them near globular glass bottles filled with water which acted as reflectors and increased the lighting power of the candle.

Candlemaking began by rendering down the tallow at first just in one pot, then by a process requiring two pots. The tallow was purified by boiling, skimming and washing with boiling water; it was then poured into a tub to cool. Wicks made from spun cotton were cut into lengths by hand on a board.

There were, and are, three principal methods of making candles: dipping, pouring and moulding. To dip candles, lengths of wick were arranged to hang from a wooden bar, sometimes held by a handle which made the whole contraption look like a garden rake. The dangling wicks were dipped into a vat of molten tallow, pulled up, straightened, allowed to cool on a rack and then dipped again. Then a 'see-saw' was developed which enabled the operator to dip many wicks at a time, using a counterweight to lift them out of the vat. Dipping machines are still used by church candlemakers.

Pewter moulds, set in rows in a wooden frame, were also used to produce candles. A cotton wick was stretched tight between two wires so that it ran right through the middle of the mould. Only tallow was used for moulding.

Wax candles, on the other hand, were usually made by pouring molten beeswax from a bowl onto wicks suspended from a frame. The wax was allowed to trickle down the wick back into the bowl. What had been poured on the wick was left to cool completely before more wax was poured on. When the candles had acquired the necessary bulk, they were given a regular shape by being rolled by hand between two pieces of smooth hard wood, wetted to prevent the wax from adhering. Beeswax, as I have said, contracts on cooling and therefore cannot be cast. Once the candle shafts had been rolled into shape, the ends and bases were shaped by pressing them against a heated metal plate.

As the nineteenth century progressed, new materials began to be developed for candlemaking. These included vegetable oils and fats, such as bayberries and candle tree berries, much used by pioneers in North America.

Another substance found suitable for candlemaking was spermaceti. This is the oily liquid contained in the huge hollow skull of the sperm whale. When one of these vast creatures had been killed at sea, its head would be removed and the precious milky spermaceti ladled out with a bucket. The finest candles were made from spermaceti, and the term 'candle power' derives from the calculation originally made as to the amount of light given by one spermaceti candle.

Michel Eugene Chevreul, a French chemist of the early part

of the nineteenth century, demonstrated that tallow could be broken down chemically into glycerine and two fatty acids, of which the most important was stearic acid. Tallow was treated with lime to eliminate the glycerine, then the fatty acid was separated by means of sulphuric acid. The resulting compound was christened 'stearin' by its discoverer. Stearin is a hard crystalline substance, of a dry texture and a pearly lustre. It turned out to be the answer to the candlemaker's problems in all respects save one. When cast in moulds it contracted on cooling and left small spaces between the crystals. This made it difficult to mould pure stearin candles. The problem was soon overcome, however, by mixing a little beeswax with the stearin and pouring it into hot moulds.

Then, in the middle of the century, the German Reichenbach developed a substance which, mixed with stearin, was to constitute the perfect candlemaking material. This was paraffin wax. It could be made from coal or peat, as well as extracted from crude oil. Reece, an inventor who had been successful in extracting paraffin wax from Irish peat, approached the candlemaking firm of Field in Lambeth, and a new kind of candle was born. 'Messrs Field,' wrote a Victorian commentator, 'have been eminently successful in their endeavours to bring the manufacture to the utmost perfection. Nothing can exceed the elegance and beauty of their white cable pattern paraffine (*sic*) candles. Paraffine, or "solidified coal gas", can be tinted to various colours without in the slightest degree losing its transparency. Two or more colours can even be combined in one candle with good effect, and they are quite as beautiful and far less costly than wax candles, which they have indeed almost superseded.'

So Victorian industry has perhaps the best claim to have developed the decorative candle. By the end of the nineteenth century English manufacturers were producing candles that were moulded in attractive shapes, along with coloured and even multicoloured ones.

Nowadays all commercially produced candles—with the exception of those used in churches, which have to contain some beeswax—are moulded from paraffin wax with about 10% stearin added as a parting agent to make the candle shrink sufficiently to come out of the mould cleanly. Church candles are dipped, not moulded. The fact that they have to be hand-made accounts for their high cost and also their superior quality. Tallow candles have disappeared, along with mutton dips; rush dips, so far as I know, are not made at all nowadays, although I have tried to revive them in this book (see Chapter 14).

The newly developed candlemaking materials were a big improvement on tallow, which had such a low melting point that candles made from it required a large wick; this went on collecting soot, thus reducing the light that the candle gave, until someone 'snuffed' the wick, cutting off its top with a pair of scissors or candle snuffers—tongs made for this particular purpose. Another big boon for candlemakers arrived about this time in the shape of the plaited wick. The braiding of this new kind of wick bent it over the flame. The wick also underwent a pickling treatment to help it to combust entirely by being steeped in inflammable liquids. The new candles would not bend over, as candles had done in the past, whether in the warm atmosphere of a Victorian ballroom or in the heat of a tropical night. Manufacturers were quick to point out these virtues and also to declare that the new candles gave a softer light than their predecessors. As the composition of the new candles was much purer and more uniform, the time they took to burn could be calculated almost exactly. A nineteenth-century manufacturer could advertise his 'Timed Safety Bed Candles' as 'prepared to burn 30 minutes only, with a view to the prevention of the dangerous habit of reading in bed'.

So towards the end of the nineteenth century English industrialists were producing trouble-free candles. It was something of a paradox that, just when the candle had been perfected, it went almost entirely out of use. It has survived, among other ways, in the form of lighting in remote parts of the country, in nightlights for children and in churches. Some buildings, such as St John's College Chapel in Cambridge, have apparently been lit principally by candles ever since they were built. Visitors to the catacombs outside Rome must still carry candles with them, just as the early Christians did. When all the other lights have gone out, the candles on the altar continue to throw out a good deal of light even in a church as vast as Chester Cathedral, as I noticed last Christmas. 'How far that little candle throws his beams!' wrote Shakespeare. 'So shines a good deed in a naughty world.'

2

The Chemistry of a Candle

When a candle burns, a number of chemical processes take place. It is worth knowing just a little about these because it will help to ensure success in candlemaking.

The most obvious feature of a candle is its flame. This burns at a temperature sufficient to melt the paraffin wax and stearin but only a little at a time. The wax that is not consumed does not always trickle right to the bottom of the candle but instead resolidifies almost immediately. If the flame were burning at pouring point, round about 132–6°F (70°C), it would melt all the wax at once, the gas given off by the melting wax would catch fire, and the candle would go up with a whoosh. Like the fat in a frying pan, wax is an inflammable material, which must be smothered with the top of a saucepan lid, a damp dish cloth, baking soda or dry sand if it catches fire. *Never* try to put out burning wax by pouring water over it; this will merely spread the fire. Instead, have at least one of the anti-fire precautions mentioned above handy. You will probably never have to use them while you are candlemaking—but they could come in useful when you set the bacon and eggs on fire!

In Fig. 1 the hydrogen gas can be seen as it is being released, unconsumed, in the gaseous chamber at the centre of the flame, A, where the wick looks black. In the luminous part of the candle, B, there is a bright luminous cone. Here the hydrogen is combining with oxygen in the air to heat carbon particles to a white heat. Outside the luminous part of the candle is an almost invisible covering of blue flame, C. Here, where the hydrogen can combine with a greater quantity of oxygen than in the luminous cone, B, combustion is complete. In addition to the flame which is burning the gas, carbon is

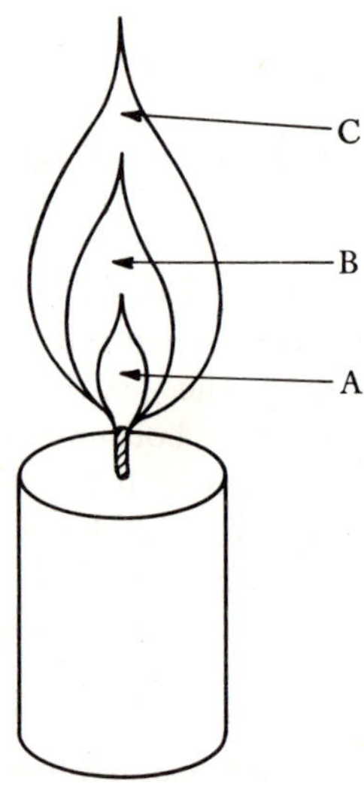

FIG. 1 Candle flame

being released from the candle in the form of soot. Normally this soot will dissipate before it reaches ceiling height, but as a precaution alter the position of your candles from time to time and do not always stand the candlesticks in the same place.

In addition, a burning candle's hydrogen gas combines with the oxygen in the air to form some water vapour, which as I have already mentioned helps to correct the dry atmosphere of a centrally heated home by humidifying it slightly.

So far nothing has been said about the heat given off by a candle. This is considerable, enough to cook on given the right equipment, and certainly sufficient to heat a food warmer.

For centuries in the Far East the thermal currents set up by the heat of a candle have been used to work toys for children. I shall make a suggestion about toys in Chapter 14 in the hope that younger members of the family, who perhaps have not grasped all the aesthetic aspects of candlemaking right away, may feel there is something in it for them.

The way a candle burns is very important. Wicks must be proportioned to the diameter of the candle in which they are used. You will find that wicks are labelled according to the diameter of candle to which they are suited. They must be large enough to accommodate the volume of gas given out by the wax. A wick that is too small cannot absorb sufficient gas to create a flame fierce enough to melt the whole width of the candle evenly. It will begin to hollow out a bowl for itself in the top of the candle. However, should you wish to make a candle that will produce its own wax 'shade' by burning in a hollow—a device which, as will be seen later on, is useful for candles that change colour—you can simply use too small a wick for the diameter of the candle. Too small a wick may also cause wax to dribble excessively; this is because it cannot draw up sufficient of the melted wax by capillary attraction to the flame, and so the unused wax pours over the side.

A wick that is too large for the diameter of the candle will make the flame combust the wax more quickly than it can be burned off at a steady rate. Lots of carbon will in consequence be released. What if you want to create a candle that—like many modern candles—is broader at the base than at the top? The answer is that you should splice a thicker wick.

Ordinary candles should not be allowed to burn in a draught (something will be said about special outdoor candles for barbecues and other open-air functions in Chapter 14). A candle standing in a draught will probably go out; it will certainly burn unevenly, and with lots of smoke, spoiling the shape which the craftsman has been at such pains to fashion. Incidentally, it is best not to blow out a candle, for fear of getting drops of molten wax over the carpet or on your furniture. Instead, extinguish or snuff it out, perhaps with a cone-shaped extinguisher. Rather than buying a candle snuffer, you can make one yourself from a piece of copper wire bent into a cone shape and attached to a rod. When this is held over a candle flame it will draw the heat from it. As the flame is not hot enough to release the gas from the wax, it will go out, due to shortage of gas. Before relighting the candle, rub a little wax into the wick to make sure that it will relight without too much smoke. Or, if the wax is still soft, push the wick into the wax.

3

Materials and Equipment

Few hobbies are quite so well catered for as candlemaking. Simply by posting an order the candlemaker can obtain all the materials he needs on his own doorstep. Candlemaking is such a popular craft that there are now many packaged sets of equipment on the market. Usually a packaged candlemaking set has something to recommend it, such as artistically designed moulds, which cannot be obtained elsewhere. Sometimes, however, the acquisition of a 'package deal' may mean that you are paying for a pretty face. The goods inside the attractive box may cost rather more than they would from one of the firms that deliver in a plain cardboard box. To avoid buying unwisely in this way, take the very simple precaution of getting the price lists of all the suppliers whose names I give at the end of this chapter. Compare what they have to sell and what it costs—remembering, of course, that you cannot really compare some things, such as the designs of two moulds, until you actually have them in your hands. Most price lists are very informative and usually illustrated so that you can see exactly what you are buying. If you are purchasing your materials in a shop, have a look, in the case of a prepared packet, at the outside of the box to see whether the contents are listed on the label and, should they not appear there, ask to have the box opened. If for some reason this cannot be done, it is worth ringing the manufacturers to find out what items the box contains. Never buy a pig in a poke.

Despite these words of warning, you will find that candlemaking is a very economical hobby. The materials can either be bought very cheaply or may lie readily to hand, since many people will have built up large stocks of candles during previous power strikes and may be prepared to sell you these cheaply or even to give them away.

The candlemaker's raw materials are wax and stearin, but there is no point in acquiring a stock of them unless you have first obtained a pot in which to heat them. It is curious that so far no wax heater specially designed for the candlemaker has appeared on the market, even though special melting units have been devised for the metal that military enthusiasts use to cast miniature soldiers. What is needed is a double-skinned jug with a water jacket and good pouring qualities, resting in a heating base and thermostatically controlled, from which the wax can be easily removed and put into moulds.

In the absence of a purpose-built melter we must make our own. Melt wax in a shielded receptacle. It should never be melted directly over a heat source, much less over a naked flame. I always use the largest sized saucepan that I can buy from an economically priced store. On the bottom of the pan I put a flat tin lid, for example one half of a shallow push-together tin box or a shallow baking tin. This is to prevent the wax melter from touching the bottom of the pan and thus being in direct contact with the heat source—which will usually be the ring of an electric or gas stove. Keep the heat very low; never turn it up full. Use a sugar or a brass-backed thermometer reading up to 240°F (130°C) to control the heat of the melting wax.

For the wax melter itself I use a 2-pint graduated aluminium jug with a good pouring spout. I keep the handle wrapped in a wet J cloth or an old cotton towel, and I stir the wax while it is melting with a wooden spoon.

The whole outfit cost me a little under £2.00, much less than a double boiler would have done. I object to a double boiler not only because of its price but also because you cannot see whether there is enough water left in the bottom part of the boiler or whether it has boiled away. Nor can I pour the saucepan top of a double boiler with any precision. The jug, on the other hand, is easy to use and is also the traditional tool of candlemakers, as can be seen from eighteenth-century prints. Although a sugar thermometer is not a cheap item, it will pay for itself by enabling you to produce absolutely controlled candlewax fillings for your moulds.

The constituents of candles are sold in either block or powder form. Paraffin wax is more easily measured and more quickly melted in powder form, and is also slightly easier to store. A bag of powdered wax can be set down anywhere, whereas block wax is best kept in cardboard boxes. Solid paraffin wax is essential for cold candlemaking. It can be bought from sculptural materials suppliers in the form of large flat cakes, shaped like the tins into which it is poured when liquid. To break up a cake of paraffin wax in order to melt it, instead of sawing it into blocks, just hit it with a hammer and it will fly into pieces.

Stearin, which is sold only in powder form, is used as a 10% additive to paraffin wax in most candles to aid extraction from the mould. Stearin is also very useful for dissolving dyes, for making candles opaque and for giving them long-lasting qualities. Recently, however, manufacturers have introduced an aerosol spray which aids mould release.

Beeswax can be bought in block form, in discs which are an inch or so across, or in sheets, honeycomb stamped on both sides, which are used by beekeepers to make partitions in hives so that the bees will spend their energies in making honey rather than wax. Honeycomb sheet is essential for cold candle-making, as are block and cake beeswax. The colour of beeswax varies, depending on whether it has been more or less refined. The sculptural beeswax is a rich brown colour which I find very satisfying as a material for direct candle construction; honeycomb sheet is slightly lighter in colour, cake beeswax more so and beeswax as it appears in church candles lightest of all. The darkest beeswax can be made lighter simply by melting it in hot water.

Besides wax and stearin, you may want to add some micro-crystalline to your candle mixture. A 1% addition of micro-crystalline increases the melting temperature of the wax and gives a hard glossy surface to the finished candle. Micro-crystalline soft is ideal for adding to wax to make flat relief mouldings. Also useful for sticking pieces of wax together is wax glue, a special tacky kind of wax.

Wicks made from cotton are essential to the candlemaker. They are sold in skeins of 3 yards (91 cm) in lengths or in rolls. Every bundle or roll is labelled with the size of candle for which the wick is designed. It is important to have a wick proportioned to the candle—unless you are trying to achieve a special effect, such as making a candle that will burn with a hollow. The usual candle sizes envisaged by wick makers are: 1 inch (2·5 cm), 2 inches (4 cm), 2½ inches (5 cm), 3 inches (6·5 cm) and 4 inches (7·8 cm), although you can make your own wicks by soaking bleached stranded cotton in a pickling solution, such as boracic acid or saltpetre, which will ensure complete combustion. However, there is no need to do this unless you contemplate making candles larger in size than those catered for by the standard wick diameters. If you do wish to make a very large candle, the simplest way of providing a wick for it is to buy a number of commercial wicks and plait them together. If you want to make a candle 3 times as thick as the candle for which you have wicks available, you can plait three wicks together.

No one is going to be content to make only white candles, so colour additives are important for the finished product. The type of dye normally used to colour paraffin wax is already mixed with wax in a *dye disc*. Manufacturers' instructions may vary, but it is usual to make up a quarter of the disc with 3½ tablespoonfuls of stearin. This is sufficient to colour about a pint of wax, or more, depending on the colour you are using. The darker or deeper the colour, the further the wax dye disc will go. If, for example, you want to turn a jug of yellow wax into a bright orange colour, a mere sliver of red dye disc will do the job. Be equally moderate when using powdered dyes. Although Dylon—a firm that produces dyes of a wide range of colours in convenient small plastic tubs—recommend employing 1 teaspoonful of Dylon Cold Dye to ½ ounce of stearin to colour 5 ounces of paraffin wax, you will probably be able to use less than this amount. Moderation will enable you not only to make economical use of the dye but also to improve the appearance of the finished candle. The darker in colour a candle is, the less it will reflect the flame. Try using just a pinch of dye until you are sure you are not over-colouring the wax.

The range of dye colours for candlemaking is enormous, and it can be increased by blending colours. Wax dye can have a little powdered dye added to it. Coloured wax can be melted with wax of a different shade to achieve a blend. 'Marbled' wax effects can be achieved by letting one colour of wax cool partially in a mould and then stirring in another colour of melted wax which has also been allowed to cool so that it will not fuse with the first.

Perfume adds a good deal to a candle, even if it is used only to neutralise the characteristic smell of melting paraffin wax, which some people do not feel is so attractive as the pleasant natural smell of melting beeswax. Perfume should be an undertone rather than an overpowering aroma. As supplied to candlemakers, perfume is oil-based and comes in small bottles. There is a wide range of different scents to choose from. A glance at the first mail-order catalogue to hand shows that the perfumes available include amongst others: hyacinth, orange,

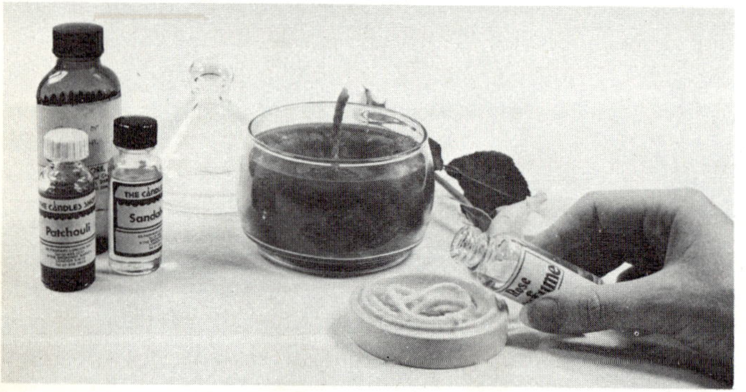

FIG. 2 Preparations for making a scented candle

pineapple, lemon, pine, rose, rosewood, patchouli, honeysuckle, jasmine, violet, amber, apple blossom, lilac, peach, musk, sweet pea, strawberry and lavender. Ready-made perfumes of this sort are extremely useful. When, later on, we come to making flower candles, I shall simply add this direction after each: 'choose a perfume appropriate to the flower and add it to the wax'.

The candlemaker is not, however, restricted to using ready-dispensed oil-based perfumes. He can make his own by macerating any flower or other scented substance he chooses and adding the material to a 'sweet' oil—i.e. olive oil or almond oil—leaving it to steep for some time. Needless to say, making perfume is just as much a craft in its own right as making candles. Some trial and error is necessary before complete success can be assured. Some perfumes are very evanescent and some flowers have to be steeped for months in oil before they impart their scent to it. If the candlemaker starts with robust perfumes, however, he will be more likely to achieve

FIG. 3 Scented candle in a glass jar (by Candle Makers Supplies)

instant success. Begin with a really strong-smelling substance, like camphor. Crumble a piece of camphor in your hands and leave it to steep in sweet oil in a covered vessel, such as a screw-top jar. Sniff the oil to see whether it has acquired the aroma. If it has, filter out any impurities from the oil. Do the same with mint leaves, orange peel and anything else that you feel has a strong enough scent to 'take'. Burn your scented candle in a round glass container with a lid (see Figs. 2 and 3); this will help to conserve its perfume.

The mould is a vital part of the candlemaker's equipment. Candles are only as good as the moulds in which they are made, so it is worth giving some thought to, and spending a little money on, your moulds to ensure that you start with the right kind. There are four basic types of mould: plastic, rubber, metal and glass—and all have their part to play in candlemaking.

Rigid plastic moulds are relatively the least expensive and have two great virtues. They have been given a good polish on the inside, which means that they will produce glossy, clean finished candles; and they are easily removed from the finished candle by plunging them into hot water. They will also stand upright without any support and are extremely long-lasting. All these qualities help to make plastic moulds a very sensible purchase for the beginner.

Flexible plastic and *rubber* moulds are essential if you wish to produce the very ornate, Gothic-style candles with an antique, hand-made look which have helped to make candlemaking such a universal craft. It is only on the embossed sides of rubber or flexible plastic moulded candles that the candlemaker can achieve an antique finish by painting on powder colour mixed with liquid soap and then rubbing off part of it to secure an attractive, time-worn surface. Because it is made of a rather fragile material which has to be pierced to allow the wick to be passed through, and because it has to be peeled back over the whole candle to release the latter, a rubber mould does not have a very long life. One way of making it last longer is to refrain from boring a hole through the tip to take the wick and instead cast the candle solid, remove it from the mould and then drill through it with a bradawl as in the method described for cold candlemaking (see p. 28). Rubber and flexible plastic moulds also need to be supported by something that will keep them upright yet not distort them while the hot wax is being poured in.

Metal moulds are slightly more expensive than rubber ones, which in turn cost more than plastic moulds. However, any metal mould is a good investment because it will last for ever.

Glass moulds are just as heat resistant as rubber ones, although they are more fragile. A glass mould offers the supreme advantage of allowing constant observation of what is happening inside. Has any water got into the wax and collected in the bottom? Are there any air bubbles? If you have any of these candlemaking problems you can see them inside a glass mould.

What about the shapes of moulds? The plastic variety usually come in severely geometrical shapes—cylindrical or square and occasionally the rounded corner obelisk type as well. Rubber moulds, as I have already remarked, are ornate. They display many well-designed shapes, some of which it is perhaps better for the beginner to avoid, but all interesting in that they stimulate not only candle moulding but also candle decoration. The embossed surfaces provided by antique-style moulds seem to cry out for gilding or painting, if not both. By contrast, metal and glass moulds are usually plain. Metal moulds provide spherical and egg-shaped candles which are very attractive to the craftsman who likes his candles to look modern.

There are quite a number of accessories that need to be mentioned before we close our list of equipment. Let us take paints and gilding media first. The traditional paints for decorating candles are dry powder colour, spirit varnish, copal varnish, white of egg, gold size, and gold leaf in sheet or transfer form. It is so much simpler to use gold transfer than sheet gold leaf that I recommend you to use the former in all candle decoration. A flat hog's hair brush is useful for laying on the first coat, while good-quality oil paint brushes of different grades should be used for the other paintwork. If you simply want to add colour to your candles, not gild them, you can use powder paint mixed with liquid soap. Gilding can be added by means of Goldfinger, a metallic finish which can be obtained in imitation silver, copper, sovereign gold and antique gold. Goldfinger is merely rubbed on with a finger, so no brushes are required.

An accessory which is so much of a necessity that it should never be omitted from the equipment with which you begin

FIG. 4 Accessories that will add panache to your candlemaking (by Candle Makers Supplies)

candlemaking is a wicking needle. With this and a bradawl you can tackle the task of wicking fruit candles with the certainty of success.

One or two firms supply wick suspension wires round which you can tie one end of the wick, whilst the other end dangles right through the candle mould and is held in a hole at the bottom. It is not necessary to buy these wires, they can be replaced by wooden cocktail sticks.

What is perhaps the most important element in a well-moulded candle has been left almost until last—mastic or mould seal. This is a very sticky substance used to seal up the hole in the bottom of the mould through which the wick emerges and is then knotted. Mastic, a natural gum obtained from trees that grow mostly in the Greek Islands, is an instant hole-stopper. It has to be handled with caution because it will stick not only to the mould but to fingers and clothes as well. Bostic Blue Tack and Plasticine are also used as mould sealers, although neither are as tacky as mastic.

If cold candlemaking is to be undertaken, several additional tools are necessary. They include a bradawl, which has already been mentioned in connection with fruit candles, a cabinet saw and a surform. Direct sculpture on wax, whether for cold candlemaking or for more ambitious adult projects, requires modelling tools of boxwood and wire. Although not essential, it is a great help to have a spirit lamp and a palette knife. You will also need a craft knife.

4

Cold Candlemaking for Children

Candlemaking does not pose any hazards for anyone who is prepared to take moderate precautions. Provided that the hot water (the use of which for hand-moulded candles is described later in the chapter) is kept below boiling point, there is nothing in the materials or methods described here that could harm any child.

Rolled candles

A beeswax sheet rolled up round a wick makes a splendid candle. Beeswax sheet is used by beekeepers and is stamped into a honeycomb shape on both sides; the usual size is 8 inches by 13 inches (20 cm by 33 cm). If you want to make a plain candle from wax sheet you can remove the honeycomb stamping by passing a heated flat object, such as a hot knife or a smoothing iron, rapidly over the sheet and allowing it to cool. Do not let the hot object stick to the sheet. The patterns on honeycomb sheet can be emphasised by cutting decorative holes in the sheet with a small pastry cutter of the kind used for stamping out petit fours.

Cut the sheet of honeycomb into the wedge-topped oblong illustrated in Fig. 5(*a*). Lay a suitably proportioned wick just inside the longer edge where the taper begins to slope downwards and turn the edge gently on to the wick. Normally the sheet should roll up just with the warmth of your hand. If it is a very cold day, however, you can lay the sheet for a moment on top of a heater, or even hold it for a second or two against the hot stove pipe of a central heating system. Then gradually roll the edge of the sheet, which has now enclosed the wick, on to the rest of the honeycomb. Make sure that the bottom edges of

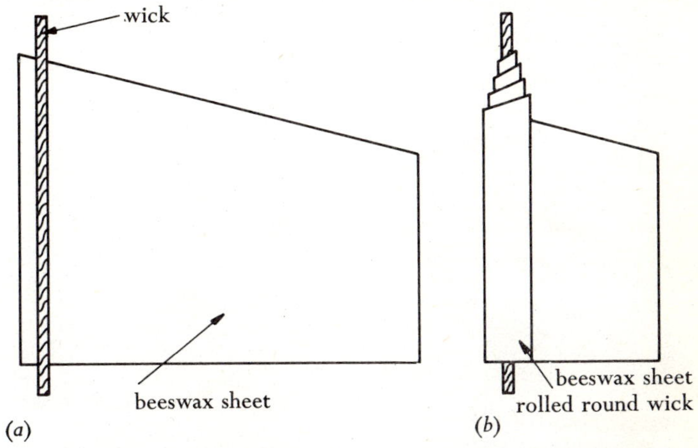

FIG. 5 (*a*) Making a rolled beeswax candle, stage 1; (*b*) Making a rolled beeswax candle, stage 2

the sheet stay in alignment so that there is a regular taper at the top. Keep on rolling, maintaining a uniform pressure, until the candle is a perfect cylinder. A beeswax sheet of the size mentioned above will roll up into a candle of about 1 inch (2·5 cm) diameter.

Honeycomb sheet can also be made into square and triangular candles. All you need is a square or triangular rod round which to form the first fold. (I used a square ivory chopstick and achieved perfect results at my first attempt.) When you have finished rolling up the sheet, press down the sides,

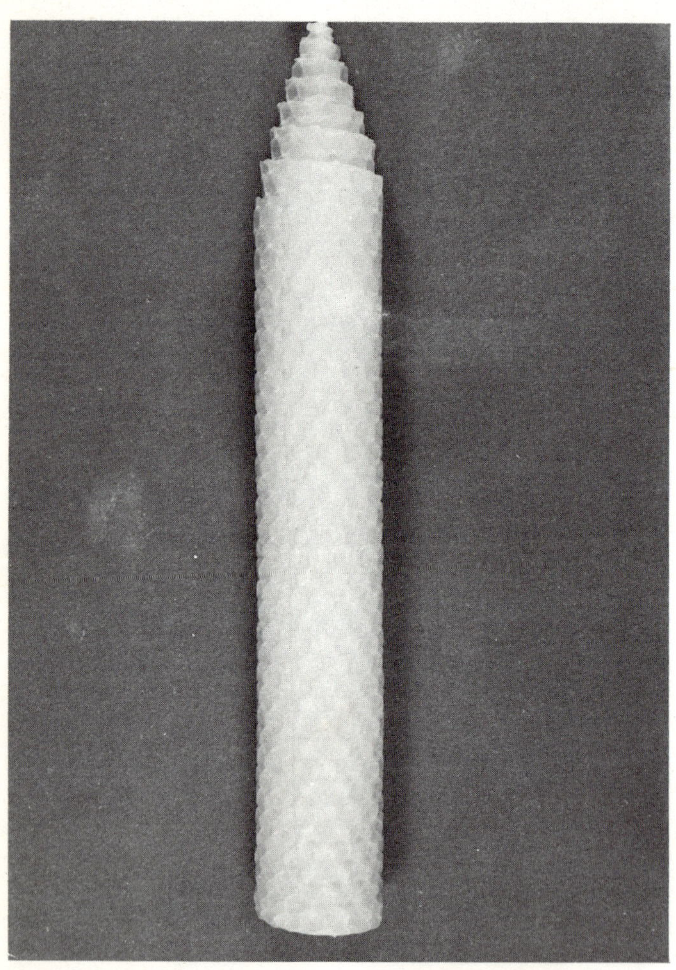

FIG. 6 The finished cold candle made by rolling up a beeswax sheet

including the tapering piece, with the blade of a knife to ensure complete squareness. Then withdraw the rod or other object carefully. The problem of getting a wick into the now empty core of the candle can be solved by pushing in a wax taper and plugging it with small pieces of beeswax at the top and bottom if it is not a perfect fit.

It is very easy to make cross-shaped, flower-shaped and star-shaped candles out of a beeswax sheet. Cut a narrow cardboard strip the height of your beeswax sheet. Lay it against one edge of the sheet and fold the wax over and round it. Remove the strip and repeat in the opposite direction so that you are left with a series of accordion pleats, all the width of the cardboard former strip, running right across the breadth of the sheet. Lift off the former and work the pleats into a star shape so that they all touch in the middle. Trim the tops of the pleats to a tapering point (see Fig. 7). Slip in a wax taper to form the core, or simply insert a wick and pack it with pieces of waste beeswax. Cross-shaped candles are made in the same way as star-shaped ones, but they have only eight folds.

Hand-modelled beeswax candles

Inevitably, pieces of waste beeswax will accumulate from the projects that I have outlined above. These should be saved and stored, for they can be used to make hand-modelled candles.

Cut some lumps of block beeswax into thumb-sized pieces. Drop these and any bits of left-over beeswax into a saucepan of hot water. The water should be well off the boil but so hot that it is not quite comfortable to plunge one's fingers into it—ordinary hot tap water will do for this exercise. Give each child a plastic spoon, a 6-inch length of 1-inch diameter wick, a boxwood modelling tool, a short length of plastic knitting needle and a pair of safety scissors.

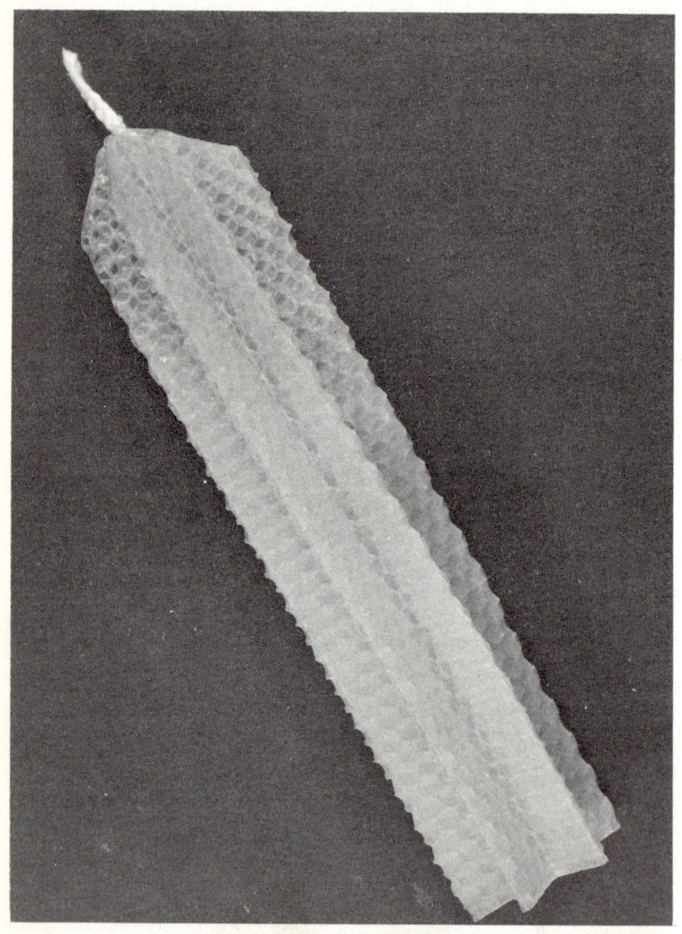

FIG. 7 Star-shaped cold candle made by rolling up a beeswax sheet

FIG. 8 A hand-modelled beeswax candle made by a child

The children must look for a piece of beeswax that has melted in the water and gone really soft. The softness of the wax can be calculated by its colour—it turns lighter as it gets hotter and softer. They remove the blob of wax with the plastic spoon and mould it round the piece of knitting needle. More bits of wax are added. Eventually there is enough beeswax on the knitting needle to mould into a candle using the fingers and the boxwood modelling tool. From time to time the candle in the making is dipped back into the hot water to soften the wax so that it is more pliable. Toadstools, gnomes, double gourds and lots of other shapes are ideal subjects to be fashioned by this process.

Pieces of wax scraped off the candle can be added to the bottom so as to give it a broad and substantial base on which to stand upright. When the modelling process is complete, the candle is held over the hot water with the stump of the knitting needle below the surface and kept there for some time to give the knitting needle a chance to warm up. The heated knitting needle can then usually be withdrawn, although sometimes a good deal of pulling and tugging is necessary. Finally, a wick is pushed into the hole left by the knitting needle.

The candle is now complete—unless, as will probably be the case, the children insist on painting their creations in appropriate colours.

An alternative method of making these candles is simply to model the wax in the hands rather than round a knitting needle. While the wax is still soft a knitting needle point is then run right through the candle to make a hole for the wick.

Saw-cut candles

One of the most exciting candlemaking projects for children consists in cutting up blocks of paraffin wax, boring a hole in each block with a bradawl and pushing a wick into the hole to make a candle.

Blocks of paraffin wax come from the sculptor's supplier in dish-shaped ingots. Fig. 9 shows how one of these blocks can

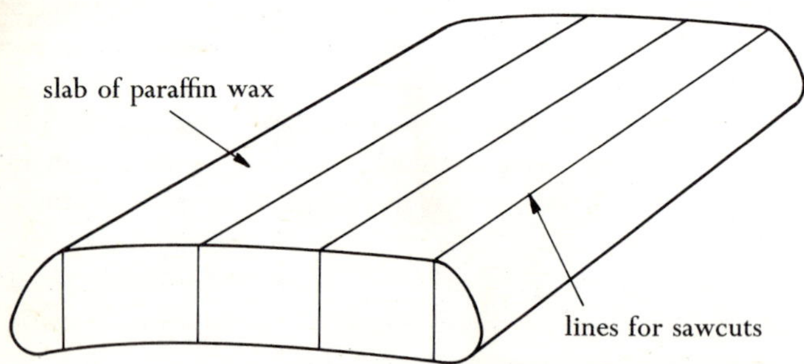

FIG. 9 Sawing up a paraffin wax slab to make a cold candle

be squared up to make it a more suitable shape for candle-making. The squaring-up process is carried out very simply by laying the block of wax on a piece of rubber carpet underlay, turned rough side upwards, and shaving away the excess material with a surform. It goes without saying that all the shavings will be carefully swept up and stored for moulding and dipping. Once the block has been pared down to a suitable shape, it can be marked up with a felt-tipped pen and a ruler and set-square into a number of oblong blocks of regular square section. The blocks are then cut out using a cabinet maker's saw or a wood saw. Next, the exact centre of each block is marked and a thin bradawl is used to drill right down each shaft, first from one end and then from the other. A wick is then pushed with a wire right down into each hole and wedged with a piece of tacky beeswax at the top and bottom.

The candle can be left with a square top, or it can be whittled to a point. Its column can be sculptured or engraved, using plastic knives and forks. The whole candle can be rounded by the same means, or with a surform.

A form of decoration that looks very attractive on white paraffin wax candles is an overlay of coloured wax film. This film is made by pouring molten coloured paraffin wax onto hot water in a pan and allowing the water to cool partially. When the wax has begun to solidify, it is removed from the surface of the water, spread out on a table and cut into equal portions for each child. The children then cut the wax film into decorative onlays, which are dipped into the water again to soften the wax before it is pressed gently on to the candle surfaces. Waxed paper (paper specially treated with wax, obtainable from bookbinders and crafts materials shops) is useful here because it can be wrapped round the candle pressed against it and held in place until it has adhered.

The blocks into which the paraffin wax is cut need not be

square. They could equally well be triangular or hexagonal. Alternatively, they could take the form of sculptured figures.

Candle painting

Although I shall have something to say in Chapter 13 on the subject of artistic candle painting, I would like to stress here that candle painting appeals to every age group. There is something about the sight of a plain white candle that makes one want to reach for a brush.

Candle paints can be made up very easily by mixing poster colour (including gold and silver poster paint) with a little liquid soap. The paint should be applied with an ordinary paint brush. And remember that too thick a coat of paint will interfere with the burning qualities of the candle.

Besides ordinary poster paint, a very useful candle decor-

FIG. 10 Quite simple ideas can enhance candles

ation pigment is available in the form of Goldfinger, obtainable in bright gold, antique gold, silver and copper. Goldfinger is simply applied with the index finger, and children in particular will enjoy smearing it on their candles. To make Goldfinger decoration even more attractive, supply the children with coloured candles (which could have been made by older boys and girls) and a number of Blic stars or other cut-out shapes, which can be bought from any stationer's or art shop. Ask the children to stick the stars on the candles and then to cover the candles, stars and all, with Goldfinger and leave to dry. When the metallic paint has dried, the children peel off the stars (the point of a pin will prove very helpful for removing any paper stars that show a tendency to stick fast) and the original colour of the candle will now show through in star shapes against a gold or silver background. Candles with gold and coloured stripes, bars or other patterns look very well.

5

Dipped Candles

Dipped candles, the oldest type of candle, are certainly not the least fascinating aspect of this absorbing craft. They have one thing in common with all the other processes. To make the best dipped candles demands careful preparation, as a build-up for the split-second timing which enters into much of the whole craft of candlemaking. There is no point in going to the trouble of mixing, colouring and heating up wax if, when the crucial moment comes and you are pouring it into the mould, you find that the mould has sprung a leak and there is no mould sealer handy. You may take the reminder I give of the need for preparation as an unwritten preface to every chapter in this book.

Select a working area for candlemaking as near to the stove as possible—this often means the kitchen table, ideal as a workbench because it is usually level. Any working surface that is on the cant will communicate its slope to your candle and cause tiltings that will ruin your coloured multilayered masterpieces.

Cover the table and the floor where you are working with sheets of newspaper. Wax has wonderful powers of adhesion; even after hundreds of years you can still see drops of beeswax on the pages of manuscripts where they fell while the priest was reading by the light of a candle. Next, put out your firefighting equipment. Although you will almost certainly never have to use it, the fact that it is there gives you a feeling of security, like an insurance policy. I have already discussed anti-fire precautions in Chapter 2, but they are so important that I shall repeat them here. If the wax in the melting jug catches fire you will need either a saucepan lid big enough to fit right over the jug and thus smother the flames, forcing the fire to go out through lack of oxygen, or a damped dish cloth, which can be thrown over the jug. Baking soda or dry sand thrown into the burning jug will also put out the fire. Never throw water on a jugful of burning wax, it will merely cause the fire to spread.

Put out on the newspaper at the far end of the table everything you will need for your candlemaking session: a measure, such as one of the tin cups used for measuring quantities in cooking; a long-handled wooden spoon for stirring the wax (metal spoons conduct heat too easily); a saucepan and tin lid; a graduated aluminium wax-melting jug (Fig. 11 illustrates the type which is useful for dipping candles); blocks of beeswax; a bag of stearin; a hammer; and a broad-bladed wooden chisel. You should also have a bag of paraffin wax because, although we will start by describing dipping with beeswax, which is more suitable for this process than paraffin wax, I shall say a word or two about paraffin wax dipping as well. You must have a thermometer at hand to test the heat of the wax, together with some J cloths, wrung out in cold water, to allow you to pick up the jug without burning yourself, a dye disc, a craft knife, a suitably sized wick, a pair of scissors and a sheet of waxed paper. I will shortly describe a holder that enables you to dip a number of candles at the same time. Meanwhile, I suggest you make your first trial dip by tying a few wicks, say three, to a short piece of wood.

Cut up some lumps of beeswax into inch-sized chunks with the hammer and chisel, placing the blocks on a piece of rubber carpet underlay. Decide on a colour for the dipped candles and select a dye disc. Beeswax has a much stronger colour than paraffin wax, which without stearin is almost clear, so err on the side of generosity when adding dye to the mixture. A quarter of a dye disc will easily colour a jugful of wax, and may even prove too strong, depending on the colour you are

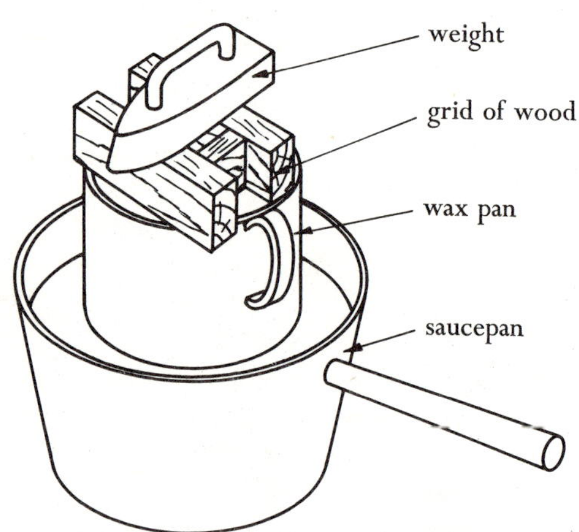

FIG. 11 Weighting the wax jug for dipping candles

using. But do remember that the dyed mixture of molten wax will be a lighter colour when cool. So cut a quarter disc from the roundel of dye-impregnated wax with a craft knife and then shave it into small slices. Put it in the jug and add 4 dessertspoonfuls of stearin.

Fill the saucepan half full of water, place the tin lid on the bottom of the pan and put the jug on top of that. The jug will probably float in the water, so cover it with the home-made grating which I illustrate in Fig. 11 and place a weight on top. The holes in the grating will allow you to add material to the jug while keeping it firmly on the lid at the bottom of the pan. When the jug is almost full of wax, which it must be for dipping, it should be heavy enough to stand on the tin lid without the weight.

The dye and stearin will melt almost immediately. Stir them well with the spoon to ensure that they combine and that the colour is unified, and then begin to add the beeswax chunk by chunk. Let each chunk dissolve before adding the next. Check the temperature of the wax with your thermometer. At no time should it be allowed to go above 180°F (82°C), which is the normal moulding heat. In fact, you may decide to dip at a lower temperature than 180°F (82°C) because the cooler the wax, the better it will adhere to a wick dipped in it. One of the secrets of dipping is to establish just what temperature will promote good adhesion yet keep the wax liquid enough to unify and not flake or scale away from the wick when cool.

Continue to take the temperature of the wax regularly. Dip the thermometer in boiling water after each reading to remove any wax and, while you do so, check that it is registering properly. If it is not, adjust your temperature readings accordingly.

While you have been adding chunks of beeswax one by one, the jug has been getting heavier and should now be resting on the lid at the bottom of the pan. You can therefore dispense with the grid and the weight. Now that the wax level is higher, add the remaining chunks of wax to the mixture with a spoon to avoid them splashing and spattering hot wax everywhere.

Since the only dipped coats you see on a finished candle are those that were applied last—the outside of the candle, in fact—some readers may be wondering why it is necessary to use coloured wax for the early dips. The reason is that when a candle begins to melt and burn down *all* the coats of wax become visible and run into each other. The candle would look very messy with inner coats of undyed wax running into the coloured outer coats.

Now cut off a 3-foot length of wick of the right thickness for the diameter of the candle—say, a 1-inch (2·5 cm) wick. Double the wick, dip it quickly into the wax so that it is completely immersed and then spread it out flat on a piece of waxed paper. Measure the height of the jug, add on 2 inches and cut the long piece of wick into shorter lengths, each of the measurement you have found. Tie these to a short length of wood. Short wicks dip more easily and keep straighter if a small weight such as a glass bead is threaded through the bottom end of each wick, which is then knotted to keep the bead in place. Dip, remove and hold in the air for 30 seconds (see Fig. 12) after which time the wax will have cooled sufficiently for you to dip again. Even with beeswax, which adheres much

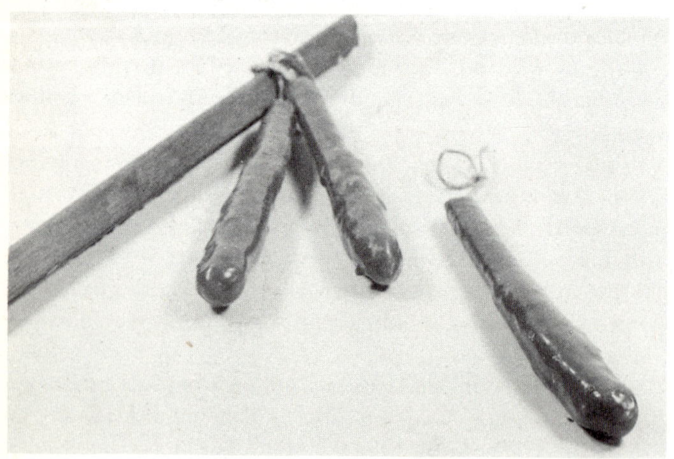

FIG. 12 Dipped candles

more readily than paraffin wax, dipping can seem an endless job. To speed up the process, use two frames; while one frame with its wicks is being dipped with one hand, the second is held away from the jug and stove with the other hand to cool.

Continue to dip until the girths of your candles begin to assume respectable proportions. As wax is taken out of the jug by dipping, you will have to add more beeswax and dye. When, finally, you are sure that your candles are the correct thickness and are satisfied with the colour, switch off the heat under the pan and cut the candles from the wood dowelling by slicing through the bottom end of the candle with a craft knife which has been standing in boiling water for a few minutes to heat it. Then cut the wick at the top end of the candle down to $\frac{1}{4}$ inch and place the candle on a flat cold surface, such as a piece of glass, a stainless steel sink unit, even a formica table. Put something else flat on top of the candle—a plate of perspex, for instance—and roll the candle into a cylindrical shape. Old fashioned butter patters, which are still obtainable from good kitchen equipment shops, do very well for this purpose. The kind that are grooved can be used to decorate the surface of the candle by rolling it between them with the grooves at right angles to the candle shaft. If the candle is rolled between two round cylinders, like rolling pins, undulations can be imparted to the shaft.

A dipped candle can also be given the shape of a stepped pyramid by dipping the centre more often than the top and the base more often than the centre. If a blob of soft coloured beeswax is hand-moulded round a wick, it can then be used as a core onto which may be added thick layers of different coloured wax. These are then cut into ornamental gouges from the outside to reveal the successive colours within.

While still warm, dipped candles can be twisted into spirals, tied into knots (a true lover's knot is very suitable for weddings) and twisted like the bars of a decorative wrought iron gate or grille. It will be necessary to dip the candle in hot water from time to time to keep the wax soft enough to be manipulated in this way.

All dipped candles will be improved by overdipping them in clear paraffin wax (without stearin) or in Chinashine at a temperature of approx. 190°F (88°C). (This temperature will vary slightly with variations in room temperature. This should be borne in mind with regard to any following temperature specifications.) Chinashine is a special kind of wax invented by Candle Makers Supplies and intended to be used as a final coat, in the same way that a coat of varnish is applied over paint. However, it is very opaque and I consider there is nothing better than paraffin wax for a transparent finish.

Dipping candles in paraffin wax does not differ much from dipping in beeswax, except that paraffin wax does not adhere quite so readily. Remember that if the wax is too hot less will be picked up, while if it is too cool it will not unify properly with the previous layer. The best average temperature for paraffin wax dipping is 180°F (82°C). When your paraffin wax candle has reached the right girth, give it an overdip in undyed paraffin wax heated to 200°F (93°C), cooling it quickly with a hair dryer afterwards. This will produce a shiny, glass-like finish.

Clear up methodically after every candlemaking session. Begin by disposing of the wax left in the jug. I take the jug out of the pan to cool and then put it back in the hot water just long enough to melt the parts of the wax touching the sides of the jug. Then I tip the wax into a cardboard box lined with baking foil and labelled with the type of wax and its colour.

Now reheat the empty jug and wipe all traces of wax from it with a piece of kitchen paper. Wax will probably have accumulated on the outside of the jug, so wipe that as well.

Some wax will also have stuck to the inside of the saucepan; deal with that by pouring out the water, heating the pan for a moment on the stove and then wiping it clean.

Put any spare wick away in an envelope marked with the wick size. Dip the thermometer into boiling water, wipe it clean and put it in its case. Salvage the severed ends of your dipped candles and store them in a box solely for wax oddments. These will come in very useful later on for filling up hollows in the bottoms of moulded candles. Put the dye disc back in its plastic wrapper, and scald and wipe the wooden spoon.

Odd blobs of paraffin wax can be removed with paraffin. Any flakes of wax which have stuck to the kitchen table can be removed by pushing them with the point of a plastic knife. Mastic mould sealer, which we have not used in making dipped candles, can be removed with white spirit, although this has no effect on those proprietary mould seals that are made of Plasticine. And do remember, when you come to use mould sealer in the next chapter, to pick what bits you can off a mould and store them in a polythene bag.

6

The Moulded Candle—Ready-made Moulds

Flexible rubber moulds

It seems a fair assumption that at least some readers will have been inspired to take up candlemaking by the sight of a superbly moulded, embossed and highly figured candle. Such candles are cast in ready-made, flexible rubber moulds and, besides being very attractive, are easy to make. So let us begin this chapter on professionally made moulds by looking at the flexible rubber mould.

Rubber moulds are made from latex and reproduce the shape of a candle to some extent outside as well as inside the mould. They mostly come to a peaked point, and even those that do not are not self-supporting. The first step therefore when using a rubber mould is to contrive a support for it. Candle Makers Supplies, who produce a wide range of flexible rubber moulds, also provide a tripod mould stand in three sizes, for small, medium and large candle moulds (see Fig. 13). These stands have metal legs with non-slip rubber feet and they can also be submerged in a water cooling bath.

Anyone intending to make extensive use of rubber moulds, however, will need to improvise a number of mould stands—unless he or she is prepared to spend a lot of money on professionally made ones. They can be very easily constructed out of oblong cardboard boxes, such as those used to gift-wrap

FIG. 13 Flexible rubber mould and stand (by Candle Makers Supplies)

bottles of wine and spirits. Cut off one end of the box so that it will stand upright. Then cut a circular opening, wide enough to admit the shaft of the mould but not the rim, at the other end. Now put the mould into the holder to make sure that it fits and that it will stand upright.

Select a wick of the correct diameter for the candle. Take a wicking needle and draw the wick through the eye of the needle, as you would a length of thread through an ordinary needle. Pierce the nipple of the peaked end of the mould with the point of the needle and draw the wick through. Tie a knot in the wick and pull on the wick until the knot has settled comfortably on the nipple, outside the mould. The rest of the wick will be dangling inside the mould. Many manufacturers' instructions state that no knot is necessary with their kind of mould (of whatever material it may be). I prefer to tie a knot to make certain, although I sometimes regret my caution when I have to struggle to untie it once it is impregnated with wax. I always keep a steel stylus handy for thrusting between the parts of the knot. Bear in mind that you should keep, until the last minute, long ends of wick at both the top and the bottom of the candle because they can be tied into loops and used to hang up candles that are to be painted or to hold candles by when plunging them into a bath of overdip. The wick, incidentally, will seal itself as soon as the hot wax is poured into the mould.

The knot is now sitting on the tip of the mould with the wick dangling inside. Take a cocktail stick, the kind that is pointed at both ends, and, holding the wick taut but not stretched so much that the peaked end of the mould is distorted, thrust it right through the wick so that the stick rests on the rim of the mould and the wick is held in a straight line down the centre of the mould (see Fig. 14). The wick is made of plaited stranded cotton, so it is very easy to push the cocktail stick through the middle. Every other candlemaker I know uses a wicking rod, round which he ties the wick, but I find it difficult to get the wick at the right tension by this method.

Now seal off the knotted end of the mould by putting a blob of mould sealer on it. Take care not to let the wick become impregnated with sealer. Mastic sealer, and for that matter Plasticine, would not merely retard the burning of the wick, it could also drop onto the candle and impair its combustibility. It is essential to seal the mould thoroughly, otherwise hot wax will spurt out of some crevice between the seal and the mould. Rub the seal well down into the mould with your fingers, and keep some seal handy to stop a leak should something go wrong during the pouring process. A flow of wax can often also be halted by wrapping around the mould a J

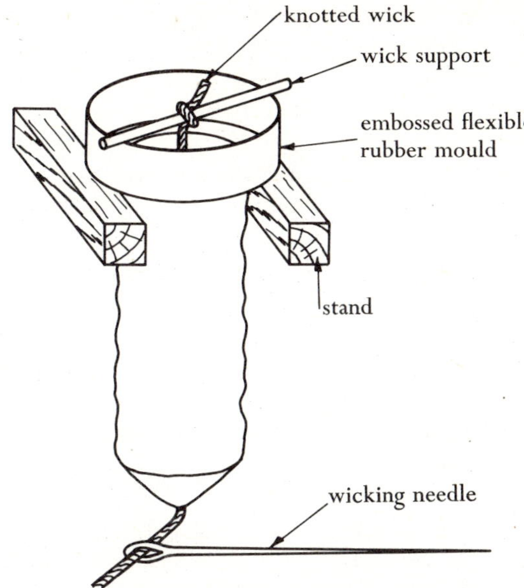

FIG. 14 Wicking an embossed flexible rubber mould

cloth which has been dipped in cold water and wrung out; this cools the outer part of the wax trickle.

Put the mould in the holder and check that it is upright. Next you have to mix up your dye, stearin and powdered paraffin wax. Use only 1% of stearin to paraffin wax, as the stearic acid will shorten the life of your rubber mould. In fact, you can substitute beeswax for stearin because one of the principal uses of stearin is to shrink the wax slightly so that the candle can be removed easily from the mould. Here the mould is going to be peeled away, so there is no need for that. Spray the inside of the mould with mould release.

Dissolve the dye disc scrapings (not quite so much is necessary as for beeswax dipping) in a little scrap beeswax in the melting jug. Now add the powdered paraffin wax a little at a time. Check the temperature of the molten wax; when it has reached 180°F (82°C), take the jug out of the pan, leave it to stand for a moment and then pour the wax evenly into the mould. Try to pour the wax down one side of the interior so that no air is trapped or turbulence created. Then tap one side of the mould with a finger to bring any air bubbles to the surface.

Put the jug back in the saucepan. Wait until the cooling wax forms a thick skin over the top of the mould and then pierce this skin in one or two places with a cocktail stick. A depression, known as a 'well' in candlemaking, will be revealed where the wax has contracted down. Top up this depression with hot wax at 180°F (82°C). You may have to do this more than once.

You must take care not to let the hot wax become mixed with any other substance, especially water. If you manage to acquire a water and wax mixture in your pouring jug the water, being heavier than wax, will sink to the bottom of the mould and you will be left with half a candle. The temperature at which wax is poured also has varying effects on the finished product. Wax that is too hot may try to penetrate the wall of a paper or plaster mould. Wax that cools too slowly will not contract sufficiently to part cleanly from the mould. Attempts to release it will prove difficult and the resulting candle will contain air bubbles, making for bad burning. Adding more stearin to the wax will aid release from more difficult moulds, such as intricate plaster ones. Too rapid cooling of the wax may produce thermal cracks in the candle.

When you are convinced that your mould needs no more topping up, examine its sides to see whether the heat of the wax has deformed the rubber. This rarely happens, but if it does, massage the mould back into shape with your fingers.

Now lift the mould, still in its stand, and put it somewhere cold to cool down. You can place it straight in a water cooling bath—a small bucket does well for this purpose—which will accelerate the cooling process and improve the finish of the candle (see Fig. 15). You can also cool it with a hair dryer, set on cold, or put it in the refrigerator. Do not put it in the freezer, however, as this could crack it.

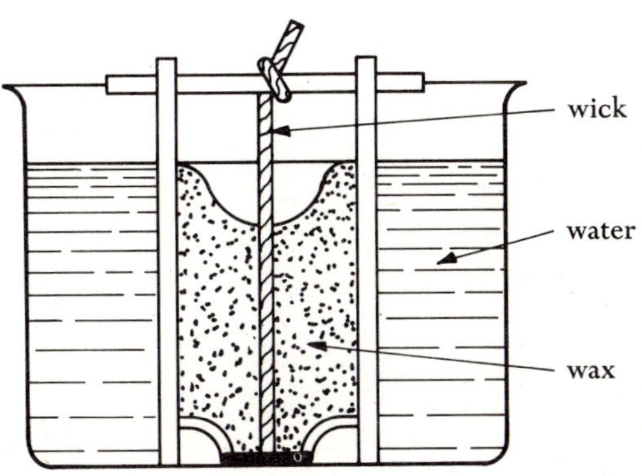

FIG. 15 Rigid plastic mould in a water bath

Now comes the moment to liberate the candle from the mould and admire your handiwork. The rubber has to be pulled back from the shaft of the candle by inching it down with your fingers. Manufacturers advocate rubbing the mould with water and washing-up liquid first. I have tried this but find that it lubricates my fingers so much that they cannot grip on the rubber mould. Instead, I just pull and, if necessary, tug at the edge of the mould with a pair of book binder's pliers, which are nickel coated and have large flat jaws. Roll the mould back on itself with great care, especially when you get to the wick end of the mould. Just before you reach the nipple, remove the mould seal and untie the knot.

Now slip the mould right off the candle, pull the cocktail stick out of the wick—breaking it in the middle to do this more easily—and level off the base end of the candle by trimming it with a craft knife right up to the wick. Scrape the edge level by drawing a palette knife across the base.

You can also level up a candle by the old eighteenth-century method of rubbing the base on a hot plate. Heat up a baking dish in the oven. Hold the candle with your fingers so that it is standing upright on the hot plate and rub it round and round in a circle. You must never, however, attempt to do this on a plate which is being heated directly from a gas or electric ring on the stove.

Now finish your candle by overdipping it in Chinashine or undyed paraffin wax heated to approx. 190°F (88°C). A final rub over with furniture cream will further enhance the appearance of the finished candle.

I consider that the heavily embossed surface of a candle of this sort cries out for decoration. Again, powder colour mixed with a little liquid soap is ideal for painting moulded candles. Do not apply the paint too thickly, however, for the non-combustible paint will retard the burning qualities of the candle. Take a clean cotton rag and rub off the excess paint from the raised surface of the candle, so that the coloured wax shows through.

Not all flexible rubber moulds are embossed; some are perfectly plain, and it is easier to remove a candle from this kind of mould than from an embossed one. Lay the mould flat on the table with its rim over the edge. Roll the mould backwards and forwards, pressing it gently against the surface of the table so that when the pressure of your hand is released it will break the suction of the rubber on the wax. When you hear a crackle, that ought to mean that the adhesion of the mould has been broken. Peel off the mould as before.

Every mould should be carefully scrubbed in soap and water after use to remove the dye and traces of wax (pink is the most persistent dye, so remember this when choosing a colour for embossed flexible rubber moulds). Once washed

FIG. 16 Two embossed candles cast in flexible rubber moulds

the mould should be dried thoroughly before being rolled back into its original shape and stored. Observe that mould manufacturers frequently send out their flexible rubber moulds stuffed and wrapped with tissue paper to preserve their shape in storage. This is a tip worth imitating.

Engraved flexible plastic moulds

These moulds, which so far as I know are made only by Candle Makers Supplies, produce a candle 5 inches (12·7 cm) high and 2 inches (5·1 cm) in diameter, and weighing 7 ounces (196 grams). With a 2-inch (5·1-cm) grade wick such a candle will burn for 24 hours. These figures are worth remembering should you decide to make candles marked off in divisions to tell the time.

The great feature of a flexible plastic mould is the shallow relief moulding on the inside which impresses itself upon the finished candle, like the fine line made by an engraving tool. All that is necessary to decorate a candle of this sort is to wipe on a little poster paint mixed with liquid soap and then wipe it off immediately, thus leaving the engraved lines filled with paint. The finished candle will give a pleasant impression of scrimshaw or of an etching transposed onto the candle shaft.

In order to reproduce the very delicate lines of the engraved pattern to perfection it is necessary to cast the candle with some precision. Mix up 22 level tablespoons of wax, 2 level tablespoons of stearin and ½ tablespoon of microcrystalline hardener per candle. The microcrystalline will bring out the fine definition of the mould and will also lengthen the time that the candle burns. Wick the candle mould as before and melt the wax slowly to 210°F (97°C); then remove the melting jug from the pan and let the temperature of the wax drop to 200°F (93°C). Put the mould on a tripod stand and warm it with a hair dryer. It is essential that the mould be supported at this point because it gets wobbly when heated. Now pour the wax slowly into the mould; this will reduce turbulence and prevent too many air bubbles from forming. Tap the mould to bring any air bubbles that do arise to the surface.

Wait 30 seconds or so until the mould feels really hot to

the touch, then transfer it to a cooling bath, making sure that the level of the water is just below the top of the mould. Top up with more hot wax when a well forms; remove from the cooling bath and peel off the mould as before.

Do not overdip the candle because this would conceal the fine lines of the engraving. Simply paint the candle as described above, trim the base and, if you want a gloss finish, apply some spirit varnish.

Rigid plastic moulds

These indispensable accessories to the craft of candlemaking are made by Candle Makers Supplies. They are available in both opaque and clear plastic, but it is far better to buy clear plastic because it is possible to see what is going on in the mould. For example, a drop of water may have entered the wax mixture, which is fatal to the candle. The best thing to do with a candle mould which is seen to contain water is to pour the mixture back into the jug and allow it to cool. The wax and water mixture will then separate out; the water will be left at the bottom of the jug and the wax can simply be lifted out. You can also see air bubbles rising inside a transparent mould. If they look as though they might persist, prick them with a wicking needle. Transparent moulds are also useful for making marbled candles. You can see the effects of stirring the mixtures of coloured wax, and also arrange chunks of wax in a pattern before pouring undyed wax on them.

A rigid plastic mould will have an almost indefinite casting life, although it can become scratched or broken if subjected to rough treatment. It has a high interior gloss, which can be kept in good standing by rubbing it with a soft cloth after washing the mould out carefully with paraffin to remove any odd pieces of wax.

Most rigid plastic moulds are self-supporting, or they fit into a base which keeps them in an upright position. This base has provisions for placing weights on it when the mould is submerged in water. However, it is a wise precaution to stick the base of a self-supporting mould down to the table with a few blobs of mould sealer in case it should tip.

I shall have something to say about the use of plastic moulds for making multi-coloured candles in Chapter 8 and will conclude here by mentioning one final advantage of the rigid plastic mould. This is that the candle can be released by simply plunging the mould into hot water. Plastic is quite a good heat conductor, and this immersion in hot water serves to break the surface tension of the wax and the inside of the mould.

Glass moulds

These moulds have many virtues. They have a rapid heat loss so that the candle cools out quickly. They are transparent, making it easy to operate inside them and enabling you to observe the effects of your work. Their high surface gloss produces the smoothest and glossiest candles. And they can easily be cleaned.

To cast a candle in a glass mould, thread the wick through the taper end of the mould. Melt a stearin and wax mixture to 210°F (97°C). Dip the wick into the molten wax to prevent it from becoming clogged with mould seal, then knot the end of the wick, draw it tight through the mould, seal it and position a cocktail stick through the wick at the rim of the mould (see Fig. 17).

Place the mould in a stand, such as the one produced by Candle Makers Supplies (which accommodates a number of glass moulds), or in a cardboard box filled with sawdust.

Pour the stearin and wax mixture into the mould; it will

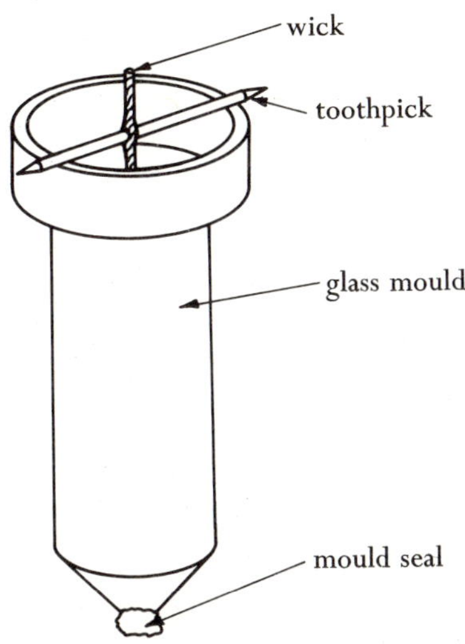

FIG. 17 Casting in a glass mould

appear cloudy at first and will then clear rapidly. Transfer the mould to a cooling bath. When the wax is cold, unpick the knot at the taper end of the mould and tap the mould lightly with your hand to knock out the candle. Should the candle stick, immerse the mould in hot water to remove the surface tension; the candle should then slip out easily.

Glass moulds have to be cleaned out, preferably after each casting, with a bottle brush and paraffin or lighter fuel to remove thin wax deposits on the inside of the mould. These will not only spoil your next finished candle if allowed to remain but also make the mould less transparent.

Metal moulds

These moulds have many advantages and are highly recommended to the amateur candlemaker who in time would like

FIG. 18 Metal mould for a cylindrical candle (by Candle Makers Supplies)

to turn professional. They are unbreakable and their life is limited only by careless use—if they are dropped, for instance, they can become dented or bent. They lose heat quickly, thus speeding up the moulding process, and they provide shapes that are unobtainable in other ready-made moulds. This is because, being made of metal, they can be cast in separate parts which are then screwed together to make such unusual shapes for candles as round tops, swelling bases, eggs and spheres.

7

The Moulded Candle–Improvised Moulds

Half the fun of candlemaking lies in improvisation. The attractions of the home-made mould, as opposed to the shop-bought article, are obvious. Ready-made moulds give you faultless performance, but you know what the end-product will be, even before you take the mould out of its wrapping paper, because you have seen a picture of the finished candle in the manufacturer's catalogue. With an improvised mould no one knows just what the end-product will look like—least of all the designer and maker of the mould! Improvised moulds constitute the artistic and experimental end of what can sometimes prove a very scientific hobby, a pastime in which adherence to a few simple rules guarantees unvarying success. There is another side to home-made moulds: they are often single-candle moulds which have to be destroyed when the finished candles are removed. This may not always be the case, but it certainly is with the first type I am going to discuss, the cardboard mould.

As there is no coming back a second time with a cardboard mould, it is worth taking care with the design and construction. Every candle made in this kind of mould is unique and you cannot make two exactly alike—unless, of course, you are able to construct two identical moulds. The design of the mould need not be as difficult as it sounds, because a great many cardboard shapes are available to the candlemaker. There are the stiff cardboard cylinders in which bottles of wine and spirits are gift-packed. On a much more domestic level there are the cores of kitchen paper and toilet rolls. Accumulate as many of these cardboard tubes as you can. Each one will provide you with a different type of candle, the bottle cylinder making up into a thick fat one, the kitchen paper roll into a long slender candle, and the toilet paper core into a short dumpy one.

Put the end of one of these tubes on a piece of thin cardboard and draw round it. With a pair of scissors or a craft knife, cut round *just inside* the line of the circle you have drawn. The disc should now be a perfect fit for the inside of the cylinder. Cut a hole in the centre of the disc using the smallest size of Xacto punch. Now coat the edge of the disc with PVA adhesive, and brush more adhesive on the inside of one end of the cylinder, about $\frac{1}{2}$″ down. Push the disc into the end of the cylinder to which you have applied adhesive until it sticks, $\frac{1}{2}$″ from the end. To engineer it squarely into place, so that it forms a right angle with the side of the cylinder, you may have to push down on the disc from the other end, using a round wooden dowel. When the disc is in position, brush more PVA adhesive around the join. The purpose of having a recess at the end of the mould is to make room for the knot in the wick which prevents the wick from slipping through the hole.

If you want to make an absolutely plain candle, the mould is now complete. However, there are a number of ways in which you can adapt the mould to produce a decorative candle. For example, cut some ornamental shapes from a piece of thin cardboard and stick them inside the mould with PVA adhesive. They will appear recessed on the shaft of the candle when it has been cast.

You could also make a candle with recessed stripes. Cut some strips of thin cardboard the length of the inside of the mould and all of equal width. Glue them with PVA adhesive to the inside of the mould so that they are parallel to one another and disposed equally round the mould. To produce a spirally recessed candle, cut out several long thin strips of cardboard, cut the end of each strip that will touch the bottom of the mould to a slant, wind each strip into a spiral and stick the strips inside the mould. Horizontal bars can be made on the shaft of a candle by cutting some thin strips of cardboard the size of the inside diameter of the mould. Glue these bars inside the mould from top to bottom at regular intervals so that they will be moulded as stripes running round the candle at right angles to the shaft.

Another idea for making a decorative mould involves cutting out with a puncher (the kind used to punch holes in paper for loose-leaf books) a number of thin cardboard spots and glueing

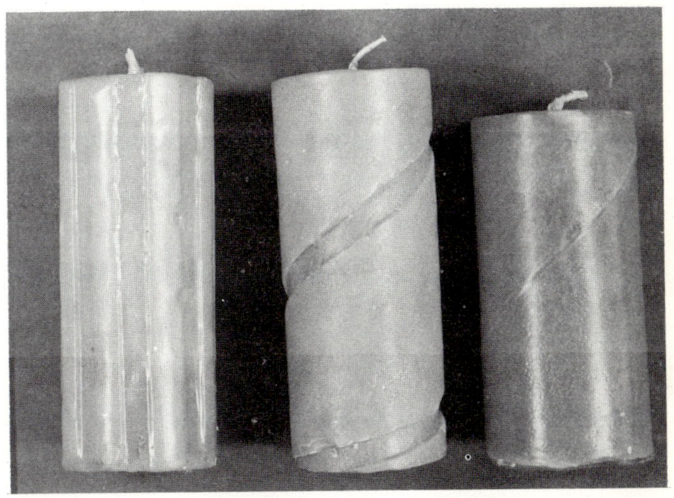

FIG. 19 Three candles made from improvised cardboard moulds

them round the inside of the mould either randomly or at regular intervals. You could do the same with ready-made shapes, such as those produced by Blic. Stars are a good shape to begin with. As a single Blic star is rather thin and so would not provide a very good recess on the shaft of the candle, stick several stars on top of one another until you have built up a fairly thick ornament. Then glue these stars inside the mould, disposing them in an irregular pattern to suggest a starry night. Cast the candle in blue wax and fill the recesses with silver Goldfinger, rubbing off any excess silver outside the stars.

If you were to pour wax straight into a cardboard mould without treating it first, the resulting candle would have a very matt surface. Wax might even penetrate the cardboard and make it extremely difficult to remove the candle from the mould. So fill up the grain of the cardboard with cooking oil or liquid paraffin (the medicinal kind). You will find that a long-handled brush will be able to force oil into the deepest recesses of the mould. Oil the outside of the mould as well as the inside. Allow the oil to penetrate the cardboard and then mould in the usual way. To remove the finished candle, cut the mould down one side with a craft knife and pull the mould apart.

Plastic cartons make very useful moulds for some types of candle. The clear plastic ones, for example, are ideal for stirring up marbled wax candles or for mixing up broken chunks of unsuccessful candles of different colours and then amalgamating them by pouring on a little clear paraffin wax.

The candlemaker should not be content, however, with using only these ready-made plastic containers as moulds. He should try to create his own moulds using different textures of plastic sheeting. You can buy plain plastic sheet, known as Plasticard, but it is much better to use some strongly accentuated sheet, such as that which makes up the bottoms of frozen food trays. To make the knobbly candle illustrated in Fig. 20, cut off the ends of a plastic food tray, roll the tray into a cylinder and cement the join with Plastic Body Putty. You can use this as a cement for any kind of plastic mould. Do not use Polystyrene cement, because this will rot the plastic. If

FIG. 20 A candle made in a mould improvised from a plastic food container

you are rolling up a thin sheet of plastic into a cylinder, attach the top and bottom with bulldog clips, and wind elastic bands around the shaft of the cylinder. To make a bottom for a mould of this type you must cut a circular disc out of plastic, fit it into the cylinder and tamp the join with Plastic Body Putty. Caulk the join well with mastic after the putty has set, just in case you have left any holes.

To remove a candle from a plastic mould which is intended to be used only once, and which in any case will be too deformed by the process of extricating the candle to use again, slit the mould down one side with a sharp craft knife—as you did with the cardboard mould—before pulling the mould apart.

There is no end to the household containers which can be adapted as candle moulds. Plastic squeegee bottles are extremely suitable, as are square cardboard milk cartons. A hunt round the house will provide a fascinating selection of plastic jars, bottles and other containers which can be converted to moulds.

8

The Coloured Candle

Colours add warmth and life to candles, and it is their bright hues, perhaps even more than their attractive shapes, that prompt people to buy candles. Coloured candlemaking is one of the simplest aspects of the craft; all you have to do to ensure complete success is follow a few simple rules.

Like perfume, colour should be used with discretion. A deep-hued candle will not reflect light back properly. Some dye colours are particularly pervasive, and a little of them goes a long way. These dyes cling to moulds and even spread all over the working surface. Pink, as I have mentioned before, is a great offender. On the other hand, these strong dye colours—pink, red, orange and yellow—are very reliable in candles. They do not even need to be mixed with stearin to ensure suspension—although, of course, you will normally want to use stearin in your dye and wax mixture to ensure that the candle comes away cleanly from the mould.

Remember, too, the warning given in Chapter 3: all powdered dyes are strong and, although a teaspoonful may be the dose recommended on the packet, a pinch will often be enough to colour a jugful of wax.

Blending colours is easy: red and yellow make orange; red and green, brown; red and blue, purple; blue and brown, black; blue and yellow, green; blue and pink, violet. There are all sorts of subtle nuances that you can obtain. Adding more stearin will make the colour lighter, richer and fuller, like gouache paint when it is mixed with white. Leaving out stearin will make the colour more transparent.

Marbled candles

There is nothing so colourful as a well-made marbled candle in which three or more colours mingle without actually blending. With a surform, cut some shavings from a block of clear paraffin wax and put them in a plastic carton. Mix one of your chosen dyes with some powdered paraffin wax in a melting jug and heat the mixture to 180°F (82°C). Pour enough of the liquid wax into the plastic carton to immerse the shavings, and mix them with a long-handled plastic spoon. Keep the rest of the wax hot in the jug. When all the shavings have taken the colour, pack them in vertical layers of irregular shape in a transparent mould. Then pour in the remaining hot coloured wax so that it amalgamates the shavings without solidifying them and forms a solid top for the candle at the bottom of the mould. Now repeat the process for the other colours you have chosen, using a separate plastic carton to mix each colour with the shavings. Pack in your colours so that at least three of them show on every side of the candle. The finished candle should have an open-textured, spongy appearance as the hot wax will have joined up with the shavings but not coagulated them.

Two other ways of making open-textured, marbled wax candles are worth mentioning. Heat some coloured wax to 180°F (82°C), pour it into a plastic carton and allow it to cool until a rubbery scum begins to form on top. Whip the wax lightly with an egg beater of the wire loop kind. Mould the wax with your fingers and pack it into the mould. Repeat using different colours of wax. When you have filled the mould with pieces of whipped wax, heat up some clear paraffin wax to 180°F (82°C) and pour it over the coloured wax in the mould. When you remove the candle from the mould, you may have to cut back the white paraffin wax coating a little with a knife to reveal the marbled colours run together but not merged to the full.

The other way of whipping, or rather frothing, wax is to blow it with a straw. It may be necessary to cut off the end of the straw from time to time and start again. Pack the differently coloured wax masses into the mould and top up with superheated clear paraffin wax as before (see Fig. 26, p. 74).

The horizontal multi-layer candle

This is one of the great favourites of the candle world. Layers of different coloured wax are arranged on top of one another—layers which can be thick or thin, according to the taste of the maker. Obviously the thinner your layers, the more colours you will be able to use in one candle. Although the layers are usually horizontal, they need not be, and I picked up a beautiful candle just the other day which had undulating green layers at the bottom, suggesting gently rolling hills in a landscape, and a light blue top, which suggested the blue skies of spring. Tiny dried ferns, stuck here and there on the horizon to look like trees, made an ideal finish to this candle.

Multi-coloured candles are best made by the mass production method, using transparent rigid plastic moulds so that you can see how the layers are forming. Wick and seal a number of these moulds and stand them close together so that spills from the jug will fall into one or other of the moulds rather than on the table. Heat up one colour of wax to 180°F (82°C) and pour it into the moulds. As the bottom of the mould will be the top of the finished candle, you should use a light colour for the first layer because it will reflect the light of the candle more efficiently and create that all important first impression.

Leave this first layer to stand for a few hours until it is almost cold. Then heat up another colour of wax and pour it into the moulds to form the second layer. In the same way continue to add layer after layer of coloured wax until the moulds are full. When the wax has cooled, remove the candles from the moulds and overdip them in Chinashine heated to 210°F (97°C).

The method that I have outlined will sound like rank heresy to most British candlemakers, although I know it is followed by many American craftsmen. Candlemakers in this country normally never pour a second layer of wax onto a first layer that has been left to become completely cold. They cool the first layer quickly by immersing the mould in a water bath,

FIG. 21 Two different layered candles made in rigid plastic moulds, together with a candle made from an improvised mould

wait until the surface of the layer has become rubbery so that it will yield but not break when pressed with a wicking rod, and then pour in the second layer of wax, transferring the mould once more to a water bath. Only by following these steps, they claim, will one layer really integrate with the next.

While it is true that hot wax poured on cold does cause a little remelting, which shows up as a matt line, sometimes accompanied by small air bubble pits, just below the line of the new colour, this defect can very quickly be cured by overdipping the candle in Chinashine. Also, cold wax will shrink, so that the next layer may overspill. This overspill, however, can usually be wiped away. It is much more difficult to follow the methods which the British technique demands—heating up the first colour of wax, pouring it into the mould, cooling the mould in water, heating up a second colour, pouring it in, cooling it and so forth. There seems to me to be no need in this particular instance to water-cool (after a pause of 30 seconds) the mould, or put in a refrigerator, or put in the cold air current from a hair dryer or fan. This does produce a glossy finish, but it is less important in a multi-coloured candle. Why not let it cool out naturally? My method does have one big advantage. It shows the candlemaker each layer as it will appear in the finished candle.

The slanted multi-layer candle

These sloping layered candles, with the levels of different coloured wax moving diagonally towards or away from the spectator, are easy to make and attractive to look at. Once again, choose a transparent rigid plastic mould, and pick a small one because it will be much easier to tilt than a large mould.

Wick and seal the mould, after pushing it into the base stand with which rigid plastic moulds are sometimes provided. Now take a lump of mould seal and prop the mould up in its stand so that it is tilted at an angle (see Fig. 22). Use plenty of mould seal for this, as it is essential that the mould is held firmly in place. Rub down the edges of the mould seal so that it takes a good grip on the table, which on this occasion must not be covered with newspaper. Test the mould with a finger to make sure it will not sway when filled.

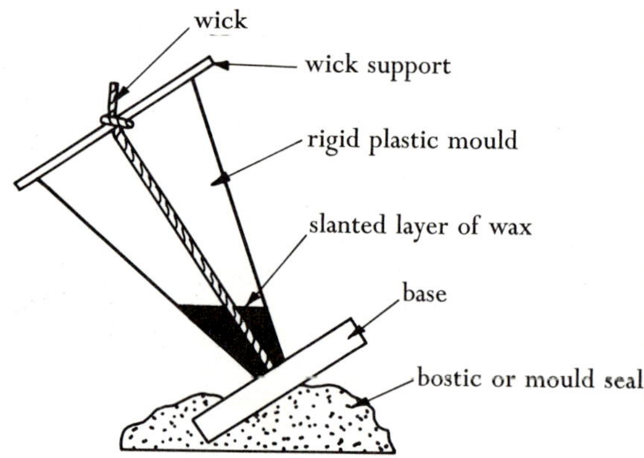

FIG. 22 Making a slanted multi-layered candle in a rigid plastic mould

Heat the first colour of wax and pour it into the mould. Let the wax cool as before—or, if you like, hasten the cooling process by using an electric fan or hair dryer turned to cool. When the layer has set, dismantle the mould seal scaffolding and set it up again, this time on a different cant. Repeat the process for each layer of wax.

Although I feel that a small, rigid plastic mould will help to ensure success with your first slanting layered candle, you need not stick to this type of mould for subsequent attempts. Any mould will do, provided that it can be given sufficient support. And one of the best ways of supporting an improvised mould, such as a plastic drainpipe or an empty squeegee bottle, is to put it in a box filled with sawdust.

Layered candles with the layers running vertically instead of horizontally are very effective, and I cannot think why, so far

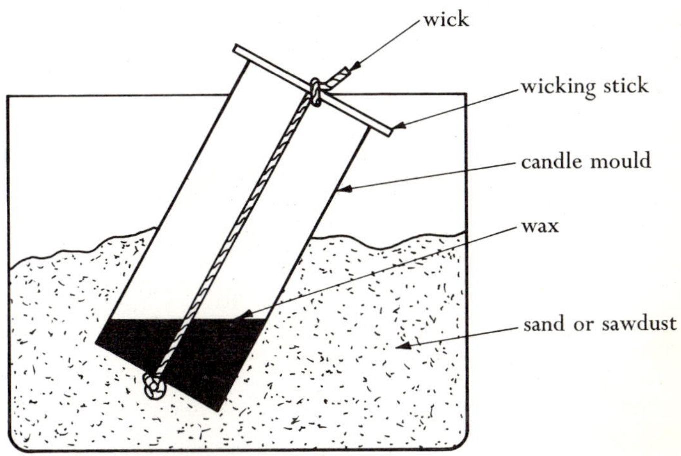

FIG. 23 A rigid plastic mould held in a sand bath for making a slanted multi-layered candle

as I know, no one but myself has made them. Candles of this sort require an improvised mould, which can be either square or rectangular. A rectangular pint milk carton, which is made from waxed paper, does very well. Bore a hole in the bottom of the carton, thread a wick through it, knot the wick and pull the other end tight through the top of the carton. Fold over the flaps of the top of the carton so that they enclose the wick and then staple them together. Cover the join and the knot with mould seal.

Next, cut a hole in one of the long sides of the carton and pour in a layer of coloured wax. Allow it to cool and add another layer of a different colour (see Fig. 24). Alternate the two colours until you have reached the top of the mould. The finished candles will have two striped sides and two all of one colour. Like every candle cast in waxed paper, it will have a

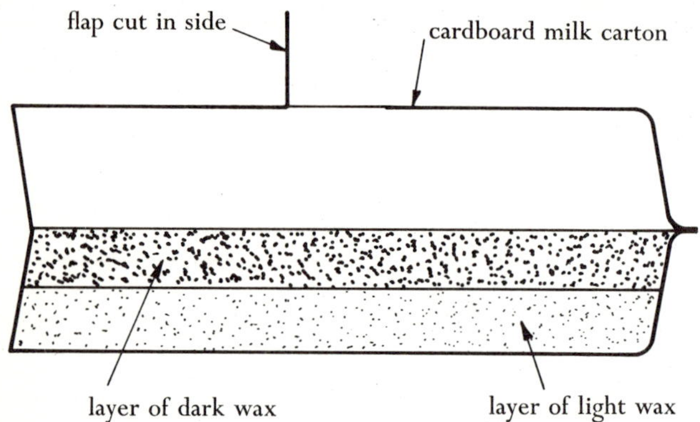

FIG. 24 Pouring the wax into a mould improvised from a cardboard milk carton

slightly matt finish. Finish it by scraping the sides with the blade of a palette knife held edgeways, by rubbing it with a little furniture cream or overdipping.

The chunky candle

Like an Irish stew, the chunky candle will accommodate all the left-overs. Cut up any unsuccessful candles into chunks. The best way to do this is to chop them into short sections with a 2-inch wood chisel, tapped down with a hammer; then turn the sections so that the wick runs vertically up and down, cut them again along the line of the wick and remove the wick.

FIG. 25 The finished vertically layered candle made from an improvised milk carton mould

Now select a square, transparent, rigid plastic mould, wick it and fill it with the chunks of wax, pressing them flat against the walls of the mould. A dab of wax glue will hold them in place if need be. Scraps of waste wax can be pressed into the centre of the mould, round the wick, to fill it up. When the mould is reasonably full and all the outer chunks are touching each other, heat some clear paraffin wax to 210°F (97°C) and pour it into the mould. It will act as a cement, bonding the chunks together. When the mould is cold, remove the candle and, with the point of a plastic knife, scrape back the paraffin wax until the chunks show up through it. Then scrape the face of each chunk so that the fracture marks on its surface disappear and it shows clean and glossy. Finally, overdip the candle.

FIG. 26 A chunky candle and a frothed wax candle

An 'instant' chunky candle can be made by sticking chunks of wax of all colours and sizes to a ready-made candle with wax glue. Continue to attach smaller and smaller chunks to the core until it disappears. Now place the candle in a narrow box and pack powdered ice round it. Pour some clear paraffin wax, heated to 210°F (97°C), over the wick so that it trickles down into the centre of the candle, bonding the chunks together. The ice will prevent the hot liquid wax from spreading out too much and spoiling the chunky shape.

Inlaid colour candles

So far as I know, no inlaid colour candles had been made before I began experimenting with them. I had learnt the technique of melting small pieces of wax and applying them precisely to a larger mass through having to repair medieval beeswax seals, a task that calls for great care and exactness. To inlay wax you require a few simple craft tools such as those used by wood engravers—gouges, chisels and a knife. Besides these you need a palette knife and a spirit lamp.

Take a square or angular-faced candle and mark on one side a decorative design. You can transfer this using carbon paper, or simply draw it on the candle with a well-sharpened Chinagraph pencil. Using the carving tools, and especially the V-shaped gouge, cut down into the interior of the design, so that it is hollowed out in a little trench dug down from the surface. Light the spirit lamp, pick up a small piece of coloured wax with the palette knife and hold it over the flame to melt. Remember that the hottest part of a flame is at the apex, just above the peak of the flame and not in the middle. When the wax has melted on your palette knife but is still a solid globule, drop it into the trough of the dug-out design. You will soon master the technique of balancing the wax on the end of the knife until it is just liquid enough to be pushed into the trough without falling off.

When you have dropped the piece of wax into the recess for the design, rapidly reheat the knife and press it down on on the wax to ensure that it stays liquid and runs into all the crevices of the cut. Continue to fill up the recess with wax until it is slightly above the level of the candle surface. Leave the wax in the recess to cool and, when it is completely cold, scrape it level with the shaft of the candle using the edge of the palette knife held at right angles to the flat surface. You should be left with a unified surface of shining wax.

Although you can fill up carved recesses of the sort I have just described simply by heating up some wax in a jug and pouring it into the scooped-out hollow, this usually results in a messy overspill, involving a lot of careful scraping away. Furthermore, you can only use one colour in one recess if you pour the wax in. With my method you can employ as many colours in the same cut as you like, blending them in piece by piece.

Besides being useful for adding colour to inlaid candles, the spirit lamp is invaluable for making running repairs to any candle. A pit caused by an air bubble (the most common fault in candle casting) can be filled instantly with a heated blob of identically coloured wax. Try to keep a little wax over when you mould a candle just for this purpose, or scrape some wax from the bottom of the candle if you have run out of the right colour. With the palette knife you can restore broken corners and contours, and seal up cracks. Often simply drawing a hot palette knife across a crack will seal it up. Scraping down the candle with a cold knife edge afterwards will restore a glossy surface to the wax, while overdipping will hide a multitude of faults.

Other colour projects

There are a number of further methods of making coloured candles. The first involves taking a plastic mould and trickling into it, at different places round the rim, liquid wax of various colours. Allow a thick trickle of each colour and then fill in the centre of the mould with clear paraffin wax. The resulting candle will have irregular vertical stripes.

Colour can be added to candles simply by painting it on (and I shall have more to say about painting candles in Chapter 13). It is also possible to apply hot, molten, coloured wax with a brush. All the great paintings of Greece and Rome were produced in this way. However, it is difficult to clean the brushes and to keep the wax liquid enough. Hot wax will not stay liquid for more than a few seconds when removed from the heat source, unless it is held in a special container like a Tjanting. This is a type of pen with a wooden handle devised for working in batik, hence its Javanese name. It has a brass reservoir to hold liquid wax, and a trickle pipe instead of a nib emerges from this reservoir. The Tjanting is dipped in the hot wax and then used to dribble a thin line of wax onto the medium to be decorated—in this case a candle, although it is also used on fabric for batik. Large, middling and small Tjantings can be obtained, and some have three pipes rather than one. Practise with the Tjanting on a piece of waste wax before using it on one of your precious candles. Needless to say, the Tjanting will only function properly when the spout is held vertically to the object to be decorated. Even when held correctly it will clog now and then, but it can be cleared very easily either by dipping it in boiling water and blowing through the pipe or by pricking through the pipe with a pricker or a piece of fuse wire.

Cold wax painting can be attempted by mixing coloured paraffin wax with paraffin (kerosene) in equal quantities and heating the mixture in a glass bowl surrounded by water. This produces a fluid, easy-spreading paint, which is much better adapted for covering large areas than the proprietary paints I shall discuss in Chapter 13.

Another technique of colouring candles which is worth acquiring is overlay. Fill a saucepan with water and pour some hot coloured wax on top. As the wax cools it will begin to form a thin skin right across the top of the pan. Leave the skin of wax to cool further, then run a palette knife round the sides of the pan to free the skin. Lift out the skin, now a round sheet of semi-cool wax, and lay it on a sheet of waxed paper. Cut the wax into shapes with the heated point of the palette knife. Place the coloured wax shapes on the candle, warming them with your hand until they hug the curve of the shaft, and finally stick them in position with a little wax glue.

All sorts of additions sculpted in wax or simply cut out of sheets of wax can be made to candles. Whether they take the form of a spiral running up the candle like a helter skelter slide, or a pair of wings, or a top hat (which can be removed to light the wick), or anything else that your fancy dictates, coloured wax accessories to the main candle enhance its appearance and attract the viewer.

When thinking about colouring candles, do not neglect the obvious. Try dyeing the wick a colour that will contrast with the main colour in the body of the candle. Why should wicks always be white? And when you come to top up the well in a candle, use wax of a contrasting colour. By doing so you will add colour to the bottom of the candle (which is the top of the mould), often the last part of the candle that craftsmen think about, and one that suffers from some neglect. Finally, when choosing a holder for a brightly coloured candle, do not put it in some drab container that will kill all the colour; instead seek one of a contrasting colour.

9

The Textured Candle

Although candles with plain surfaces—which are so suitable for ornamentation by painting, inscribing with Tjanting pens and applying wax shapes, Letrafilm decoration or Letraset inscriptions—will always have their admirers, many candlemakers regard the surface texture of the candle as all important. There are various methods of texturing candles, but they can be classed under two main headings: moulded decoration texture and hand-worked texture.

Let us look first at moulded texture because it is the easiest to apply. Wax is a very delicate moulding medium and takes on the impression of anything with which it comes into contact, even reproducing grains of dust on the inside of the mould. It can consequently be made to acquire almost any texture.

Some textured materials, like Hessian wall paper, will need to have their grain filled up before they can be used as moulds so that the wax does not penetrate into them. So it is obviously more convenient to use close-textured materials that can be built into moulds without any preliminary treatment. High on the list of suitable substances comes plastic. The wide use of stressed plastic for packaging goods means that there is a wealth of interesting textures available which can be turned straight into moulds, following the method I describe in Chapter 7. Don't forget that the shinier the surface of the plastic you are using, the more cleanly moulded and glossier your candle will be. Do not neglect the rougher plastics, however, used for ceiling tiles and wall panels. These are now being produced in the most attractive textures and patterns, and if you want to construct a candle that looks as though it were made out of stones cemented together, make a mould from pieces of the underside of decorative tiles or facings.

All sorts of natural textures can be imitated on the surfaces of candles. Make up the four sides of a plastic mould as described on pp. 62–3, but before you stick them together paste onto the inner surfaces natural objects such as dead leaves and twigs, bark stripped from an old tree, feathers or grains of sand. Paste them down with PVA adhesive and leave the parts of the mould to dry. Then stick the four sides together with Plastic Body Putty and tape the mould with adhesive tape to preserve its shape while it dries.

If you were to cast from this mould as it stands the likelihood is that at least some of the lining would become permanently embedded in the wax. Avoid this probability by brushing polystyrene varnish over the inside of the mould. You will lose some definition, but this is preferable to spoiling the candle. Allow the varnish to dry and then cast in the usual way. Take care in pulling the pieces of the mould apart.

You can use the same technique of giving body to the mould lining when making paper moulds—particularly those made from wallpaper with textured surfaces.

Hand-worked texture is fascinating to apply. Probably the best-known technique in this type of decoration is 'percussion bulb'. When any crystalline substance—and this includes paraffin wax—is struck a sharp blow with a rounded or flat-faced instrument, a small saucer-shaped mark is made. Of course, if too much force is used in applying this blow, a fracture may result. To texture the surface of a candle by this method, simply remove it from the mould and tap the shaft with the head of a small hammer. Different impressions can be created by using hammers with different heads, made from rubber, plastic or wood. Try using a hammer with a distinctive pattern, such as the wooden ones sold in kitchen equipment shops for softening steaks.

Texture can also be imparted by hand to a candle by scraping and carving it while the wax is still fairly soft—and even when it is hard. Steel tools are likely to make deep gashes in the wax unless you handle them very carefully, so it is best to use plastic cutlery or boxwood modelling tools. The tines of a plastic fork, for example, will render a delightful wavy line pattern on the surface of a plain candle.

You can achieve other effects by treating the candle surface while it is still reasonably warm. For instance, wind a cord round the shaft from top to bottom and leave it until the candle is quite cold. Or wrap the candle in a textured material, such as Hessian wallpaper. Or roll it between two patterned wooden objects, like butter patters.

Various metal shapes can be impressed on the surface of a still-warm candle, especially if the metal is warmed up first. Do this with monograms or double initials which can be cut out of type metal, or any other soft metal, and then stamp all over the surface of the candle. The metal stamp should be attached to a wooden handle with epoxy adhesive. Rock the stamp on the candle shaft so that it imprints its full surface on the wax. All sorts of sculptural shapes can be impressed on candles while the wax is soft. For example, a broken cameo, the head of which is still intact, can be fixed to a wooden handle and then pressed into the surface of a candle (preferably one with flat sides) so that it gives an impress in itaglio.

Much can be done to create different textures by experimenting with temperature control and trying to build into a

FIG. 27 A layered candle can be varied in texture as well as colour

candle the faults you have been advised to avoid so far! Take air bubbles, for instance. I have suggested that you try to get rid of these by tapping the candle mould to make them rise. Instead of eliminating them, why not induce them by whipping up the wax with a whisk before you pour it into the mould or by blowing down a straw dipped in the mould, as I have suggested in the previous chapter? This will give the candle a honeycomb texture like a Gruyere cheese. When you have finished blowing, however, you may have to leave part of the straw in the wax.

Allowing the candle to cool slowly leaves it with a slightly pitted surface, while rapid cooling in a water bath produces a more unified surface. If wax is poured at a temperature below 180°F (82°C) a marbled surface will result. This can look rather attractive when it shows up against a dark colour, or several dark colours which give the candle a marble-like appearance.

To produce small bubbly lines encircling the candle, put it directly into a cooling bath in which the water level comes only part of the way up the candle shaft. Then immerse it successively deeper, to get a number of rings up the candle shaft. A roughened surface will also result if you pour hot wax on top of cold wax in a mould. The hot wax will remelt the layer below it, making a 'ring' around the candle. Cooling a mould very quickly by, for example, putting it straight into a refrigerator at a very low temperature, or a freezer, or into a bath full of ice cubes may give the finished candle a delicately cracked appearance, like old Chinese porcelain. Pouring wax into a mould when it has just begun to solidify can also produce strange effects.

FIG. 28 A plain candle enhanced by overdipping

Let us not forget, in conclusion, the various proprietary finishes for candles available to the candlemaker. Just as too much stearin will produce a chalky crystalline finish, so the right amount gives a well unified surface. Microcrystalline hard granules improve wax structure when as little as 1% is added to the mixture. Microcrystalline soft granules help to give the right surface to flat relief mouldings. Chinashine, as mentioned before, is very useful for overdipping wax and acts in the same way as a glaze for porcelain or pottery. Possibly the perfect finish is an overdip in clear paraffin wax heated to 190°F–230°F (88°C–122°C). This enhances the appearance of the finished candle and removes any surface imperfections such as pits, mistakes in carving and so forth.

10

The Sculptured Candle

Making sculptured candles is undoubtedly the most artistic and rewarding side of the craft. A single carved or sculptured candle, or a short run of candles produced from a hand-modelled original master, has the quality of being individual as well as being a fascinating test of the candlemaker's skill. If you sculpture your candles or make your own master moulds, there is no danger that your work will ever be confused with that of anyone else, whereas all candles turned out from a ready-made mould look very much the same.

It is, then, all the more surprising that sculptured candles are so rare. I recently viewed several collections of home-made candles and did not see a single sculptured or carved candle. It seems to be virtually a monopoly of the professional candlemaker.

This neglect of the sculptured candle does not lie in its difficulty. There are about half a dozen ways of making them, of which at least one will surely recommend itself to the home craftsman. You do not need to have a formal training in art or a great talent to make a sculptured candle. Often you can canalise other people's genius into your candles. One of my most successful candles, for example, was made by impressing a nineteenth-century Neapolitan cameo into the face of an octagonal candle. The result was a beautiful rendering of the cameo in wax. I could also have utilised this cameo by making a plaster mould of it and then pressing this mould onto a strip of clay. The clay would then be coated with Wubastuf (a process which I shall describe in a moment) and turned into a flat flexible rubber mould. This would be filled with a shallow depth of hot wax, which finally would be wrapped around a circular candle.

Enough has been said to prove my point. Even if you do not feel that you are the world's greatest sculptor you can still obtain a master of some sort from which to cast sculptured candles. Of course, as the master will be your choice, the candles will remain individual.

The simplest yet perhaps the most satisfying way of sculpturing a candle is to make a bas relief block candle from beeswax. Select a large block of beeswax—or, if necessary, melt some beeswax into a suitably sized block, adding colour if you wish in the process. As untreated beeswax is a rich dark brown and melted beeswax a paler cream colour, you had better decide at this point whether you are content with these colours or, if you are not, whether you are going to add colour now or wait and dip the finished candle in coloured wax, or simply varnish it.

I have assumed that you will want to make your first sculptured candle in beeswax rather than paraffin wax. Beeswax offers greater flexibility, is much less likely to chip and crack than paraffin wax, and is easier to work.

Saw up the beeswax into a suitably sized block if you are working with lump beeswax. An ordinary cabinet maker's saw will do quite well. Drill a hole with a bradawl in the middle of the block and wick the candle by threading through a suitably proportioned wick on a wicking needle. Inserting the wick at this stage means that there will be no need to handle the candle unduly after the carving has been completed and thus to risk spoiling the finished job.

To sculpture the candle you will need some sculptor's modelling tools, which consist of boxwood spatulas with ends shaped into curves, points and serrated edges, and short boxwood rods with looped wires twisted into different shapes. Both kinds of tool are extremely useful, the spatulas for rendering definition and texture, the looped ones for taking off scrapings of wax a little at a time. One of the merits of the wire tools is that they can be heated up by plunging them in boiling water, thus enabling them to cut through wax more easily.

As I have said, a bas relief is an ideal project with which to begin, because the amount of carving needing to be done is minimal. The beeswax block will provide the main mass of your sculpture. All you have to do to decorate it is a little shallow relief carving. Start work by laying the block on its side on a sheet of rubber carpet underlay, with the rubber side uppermost. On this springy base you can press down on the candle without fear of damaging its underside. Draw a margin to each side of the block, within which your bas relief sculpture will be enclosed. Outline the margin clearly with the point of a modelling tool and then use the same tool to scratch on the wax a rough sketch of what the finished decoration will look like. You can, of course, make a preliminary rough drawing of this to size just to help you with the carving. Now use the point of a wire loop to scrape out a little wax, cutting back the hollows from the main masses of the sculpture. If you are sculpturing a figure, use the boxwood spatulas for defining the lines of the hair, rounding the limbs and putting in the expression of the eyes. Since this is going to be a one-off sculptured candle, not a master for a mould, you can undercut as much as you like, leaving detached arms and so forth, to produce a feeling of depth. As you scrape off pieces of wax, lay them aside on a sheet of waxed paper. They will be useful for adding relief to those parts of the work that will protrude from the mass, such as the horns of an animal or the nipples on the breasts of a goddess. Check that the margin is evenly drawn. Instead of leaving it plain you can ornament it by pressing into it some object that will mark it with a pattern. Something very simple, like the milled edge of a coin, can be used for this purpose to good effect.

When you have completed the sculpturing of the bas reliefs to your satisfaction, you may decide to leave in all the marks your tools have made in creating the carving, thus giving the finished work a fine appearance of professionalism. Alternatively, you can smooth them out—perhaps just in the background—by rubbing them with a round-ended modelling tool.

Now comes the question of the final finish. Dipping the work in superheated wax or in Chinashine at 210°F (82°C) will put a gloss on the finished candle, but it may also conceal some of the definition you have put into the carving. Why not leave the sculpture as it is, or simply varnish it either with spirit varnish or with the wax varnish that picture restorers use? Some kind of varnishing does help to protect the sculpture from dust—the great enemy of candles—because, although it is meant to be burnt, you will probably want to keep it about the house for a time to show your friends. Wax sculptures of this sort last practically for ever, and a number of them have survived from the Middle Ages.

It is a small step from carving a bas relief on a square block of wax to sculpturing a free-standing figure. Once again, use beeswax, and work this time from a rectangular block which will give you the proportions of the human figure—a block six times the measurement of the finished head. Drill the block with a bradawl and wick as before. Cut a little hole around the bottom of the wick in the base of the figure and push the knot of the wick well in so that it does not protrude and make your candle wobble. It may help, while modelling the figure, to stick the block with wax glue onto a small square of wood; this will raise it slightly above bench level. Remember that the line of the wick will have to run down the main axis of the figure and that, if the legs are to be parted, then the wick will have to run down the middle of one leg. It is better to side-step this difficulty, on your first attempt at least, by sculpturing the figure with the feet placed together.

When sculpturing the figure, do not rely solely on the modelling tools but cut off fairly large chunks of wax with a piercing saw. Work the saw very carefully, however, in case it should stick. You can also speed up the carving process by rounding off corners and making V-shaped incisions with a craft knife. Any rough edges that are left can be smoothed away by rubbing with a round-ended modelling tool. Leave the bottom part of the block of wax as a plinth for the figure to stand on. Try to disguise the wick at the top of the figure by smearing it with beeswax and plastering it down close to the head, since if it sticks up straight in the air it can make the figure look rather grotesque.

The finished figure can be varnished and then painted in realistic colours, following the method described in Chapter 13.

It is a very easy transition from the monolithic sculptured candle, carved from a single block of wax, to the statue candle in which parts of the figure are carved separately and then stuck onto the body with wax glue.

Paraffin wax sculptures look just as effective as beeswax ones, but the material lends itself better to broad outlines than to finicky detail. Use it for carving bold, abstract sculptures with sharp angles rather than delicately modelled representational ones. The translucent qualities of paraffin wax, cast with only a little stearin so as to be semi-transparent, can be enhanced by setting the sculpture on a plinth with a ground glass top and a bulb underneath so that the whole figure is lit up.

Let us now move on from carving to modelling, following the instructions given for shaping beeswax in Chapter 4 on cold candlemaking. Modelled accessories enhance candles which are in the main cast blocks.

One kind of direct modelling which ought to be attempted by every candlemaker, and which can be carried out in paraffin wax, beeswax or modelling wax, is the working up of shapes from flat sheets. The most obvious outlet for flat-sheet work is making flower candles, in which the candle simulates a blossom standing in a vase. The centre of the candle, comprising the stamens and petals, can be made from thin paraffin wax sheet, beeswax sheet or even sheet modelling wax. Modelling wax is not normally used for candles, but in the case of a flower candle the wick is replaced by a commercial wax taper, which will supply all the fuel required. When the taper is lit, the modelling wax petals and leaves, having served their decorative purpose, will simply melt and fall away. Paraffin wax sheet can be made by pouring coloured hot liquid paraffin wax onto a flattened out sheet of wax paper and allowing it to cool.

Begin assembling the flower candle by dipping a wax taper in liquid wax of the same colour as the flower. The taper should run right up into the heart of the flower, where its end can be disguised as a stamen. Form the petals by cutting up wax sheet into appropriate shapes. To ensure that your petals and leaves are shaped properly, have to hand an example of the flower you want to imitate. Pull the petals off so that you can copy their shapes. You can produce ready-moulded leaves by making a plaster mould of a leaf from the flower model. This is done by placing a leaf with its top side uppermost on a piece of waxed paper and sticking it down with PVA adhesive. Pour plaster of Paris on the leaf and leave it to dry. All that remains to be done to produce a wax model of the leaf is to grease the inside of the plaster mould with liquid paraffin and then pour in a little suitably coloured wax. Stems can be made by taking some semi-cool wax and rolling it out between your fingers and the top of the table. Soften the ends of the stems with your fingers before moulding them to fit the main stalk of the flower. Press the petals and leaves onto the stalk or the stems and stick them down with wax glue if they seem unwilling to join. Paint the joins so that no uncoloured wax glue appears. Add a perfume appropriate to the flower to the wax that is being rolled out and moulded. (See Chapter 3.)

Flower candles probably look their best in a real flower vase containing a little water to support the candle and ensure that it does not burn right down to the bottom of the vase, where it might smoke. If the vase used is a pottery or porcelain one, burning a flower candle in it presents no real problem. If it is a glass vase, however, the heat from the candle may crack the vase. So make sure that the vase is well filled with water, or place the candle first in one of the toughened, heat-resistant glass containers that Candle Makers Supplies produce specially for perfumed candles. Whatever kind of vase you employ, it is a good idea to anchor the bottom of the candle firmly to the bottom of the vase with a little mould seal before adding water.

One of the most attractive forms that a flower candle can take is that of a lotus flower floating on water and surrounded by its spreading leaves. The water container can be a simple pottery bowl or an elaborate cut-glass dish, the facets of which will reflect the light of the candle. The centre of the lotus can be made rather solid, with lots of petals, to prolong its life.

Inevitably, the candlemaker will want to produce sculpted candles that he can repeat by casting, especially when one of his creations is so admired by his friends that they want one just like it for themselves. The material from which a master model can be made depends on the substance in which the mould is to be cast. If the mould is to be made of plaster of Paris, it is possible to use Plasticine or modelling clay for the master model. If, on the other hand, it is to be cast in Wubastuf—a liquid moulding material which can be painted on the model without prior heating or melting and which gives a high degree of definition in reproduction—the master can be made of the following: plastic (such as that provided in plastic modelling kits), wood, glass, porcelain (figurines which you have always admired and which you can cast as candles), plaster of Paris, clay and stone (either a piece of soapstone that you have carved yourself or some stone object that you have 'found').

Let us take the plaster of Paris method first. Make a small sculpture in Plasticine or clay. Brush it with liquid paraffin and sink it down into a plastic or cardboard box exactly half filled with freshly mixed plaster of Paris (mixing plaster of Paris is described in detail in the following chapter). Avoid figures that require a three-part mould.

Before the plaster has quite dried, cut holes in each corner of this bottom half of the mould with the point of a palette knife. Now leave the plaster to dry completely and then brush the top of the mould with liquid paraffin. Freshly mix enough plaster to fill the top half of the box, and pour it in. The plaster will set into the holes you made in the bottom half of the mould, leaving four register marks to enable you to fit the two halves of the finished mould together exactly. Allow the plaster to dry. Remove the mould from the cardboard or plastic box—to do this you may have to cut it with a craft knife—and cut a pour hole and an air vent in the sides of the mould. Both holes should be positioned inconspicuously so that the flash marks they make on the finished candle can be trimmed off without leaving unsightly traces. Now gently lever the two halves of the mould apart with a wooden chisel and remove the model. Finally, grease the inside of the mould with liquid paraffin before pouring in the wax.

You have already encountered the flexible rubber mould when casting candles from professionally made moulds. This type of mould will peel back from virtually any shape of master, but the more streamlined the master, the less the difficulty experienced in removing the mould both from the master and from candles made in it. The master must be made from clay or one of the other substances listed above, and any gaps between, say, the arms and the body must be filled in with clay so that the master stands as a monolithic figure. Stick the figure down to a square of wood so as to give it support while you work. Heat the master gently with the hot air current from a hair dryer. Put just enough Wubastuf into a container to allow for displacement and dip the master in. Remove the master and hold it over the container until it stops dripping. Then heat the master with the hair dryer once more to hasten setting. Blow away any air bubbles to avoid a pock-marked mould, and refrain from touching the setting Wubastuf because this could spoil the finish. Setting will take several minutes. When the Wubastuf has changed colour from white to off-white, dip the master into the liquid Wubastuf again. Continue dipping until you have a smooth, even coat of Wubastuf, about $\frac{1}{16}$ inch or more thick—the colour change will occur with each dipping but will become less pronounced. The larger the master, the thicker the coating of Wubastuf should be. Have a look at some of your ready-made rubber moulds to gauge how thick the mould ought to be. Leave the mould to cure in a warm place for 24 hours before trimming off any ragged edges.

Remember my original suggestion for Wubastuf: that it can be used to make a flat relief mould to produce layers of wax which can be wrapped round candles. Use clay for the master and pour a thickness of $\frac{1}{8}$ inch of Wubastuf over it, swilling it around to ensure an even coating containing no air bubbles. Again the master should be left in a warm place for 24 hours until cured and almost transparent. Set particles of Wubastuf that find their way into the liquid could cause faulty moulds, so do look out for them when you are pouring.

A fascinating method of producing sculptured candles, which so far as I know has never been tried in this country, is to carve a mould in two halves out of soapstone. You need two flat pieces of soapstone of the same size. The best way of obtaining them is to saw a block of soapstone down the middle, using an ordinary wood saw. File two nicks on the top and bottom of the block before you cut it to ensure that the blocks register when put together as a mould. The nicks can be used to hold string which will bind the two halves firmly together. On the middle of one block, draw out a silhouette of the shape of the candle. Carve out the depth of the mould with wood carving tools until you have dug out half the body of the candle. Now coat the flat parts of the block with ink and superimpose it on the other block. The part of the block that is not covered with ink indicates the area that you must carve out to make the other half of the mould. When you have finished carving, cut a channel for pouring in the wax and a substantial air vent. As soapstone becomes harder the more it is exposed to heat and also greasier through contact with wax, your mould should never wear out, nor give you any troubles when releasing the candle.

11

Casting from Natural Objects

Nature offers a wealth of shapes to the candlemaker. If the number of candles made in natural shapes is anything to go by, this is one of the most popular aspects of candlemaking.

There is no difficulty about making candles in the shape of fruit, or any other natural shape, provided that you follow closely the few simple steps outlined here. The first step is the selection of a suitable object. Many natural objects are intriguing sculpturally but present casting difficulties. A coconut has an exciting shape but is covered with long hairs which are bound to become incorporated in the plaster of the mould and make it difficult, if not impossible, to remove the model.

Choose something hard, smooth and with no undercuttings. The thing which you are going to cast must not have any turned down corners (as is the case with an opened pine cone, for example). Nor should it have stalks which terminate in a hook (as with a green pepper). If you particularly want to cast an object that has undercuttings or cavities, fill them up with wax or Plasticine before you cast it. If you choose to cast a fruit with a twisting stem, first cut off the stem and, if need be, cast it separately. The harder your original model is, the better. Wax fruit makers in Victorian times, whose craft has an obvious affinity with the making of fruit candles, used to advise beginners to start with an egg—hard-boiled. Any hard fruit or vegetable, such as a gourd, will do to start with.

First check the model for twisting stems or cavities, then estimate the size of the box which you will need to cast it in. An ideal casting box is one of the plastic punnets or square boxes used to pack a wide variety of soft fruits. Select one of suitable size, brush your gourd or other hard fruit with a little cooking oil and set it aside for a moment.

To cast you need plaster of Paris. This is best bought in a 7-pound bag and many wallpaper shops and decorators supply it in this size of package. You will never need as much as 7 pounds for one casting, but it helps to have a reserve supply of plaster in case of emergencies. To mix plaster of Paris you need water, a large plastic bowl and a wooden spoon. The water is best held in a large jug kept full to save you having to keep running to a tap. Any plaster not used for casting will harden after it has been made up and set solid. To remove old plaster from the bowl, bend the bowl slightly in your hands and the plaster will break away from the sides. To clean the wooden spoon, scrape it with the point and edge of a palette knife.

Begin the casting by mixing enough plaster to fill half the small plastic box which you have chosen as the casing for your mould. You can calculate approximately how much plaster this will be by half-filling the mould box. Plaster of Paris expands somewhat and occupies slightly more space wet than dry. Now pour ½ pint of water into the plastic bowl. Pick up the plaster in your fingers and sift it onto the surface of the water, swirling your hands around so that you cover the whole surface. Before long, the thick and creamy appearance of the liquid plaster will tell you that it has begun to set. Stir it vigorously with the wooden spoon to expel air bubbles and pour it into the box until it is half full. The setting time for plaster depends on the temperature and on the proportions of plaster to water. Allow between 5 and 15 minutes for the plaster to set; 15 minutes is the very longest that the plaster will take to set and any casting that you have to do must be made before it does. Do not make the plaster too thick; otherwise it will not be liquid enough to penetrate the crevices in the casting. On the other hand, do not make it too thin, because it will not set properly and will be porous and friable, and likely to break up when you are removing the model from the casting box.

Take the gourd, or whatever else you are casting, and push it gently down into the bath of plaster until it is exactly half submerged. Unless you hit the halfway mark exactly, part of the mould will be undercut and, when you come to pull out the model, it will break the mould. Usually you can judge the halfway mark of a small object such as a fruit by eye. If you have any doubts, draw a line with a fibre-tipped pen round the meridian of the fruit. If your fruit is dimpled, like an apple, cast it with the dimpled side down. If you cast it sideways, you will break the mould.

Allow at least an hour for the plaster to set. Indeed, it does no harm to leave the plaster to set overnight to ensure that it has dried out completely before you pass on to the next step. Before the plaster has hardened, however, take the point of a palette knife and twist it round in the empty corners of the mould until you have made four hollows. Plaster poured into the top half of the mould will set into these hollows and give you four register marks which will enable you to fit the two halves of the mould together exactly.

Mix the same amount of plaster as you did before, leave it to crystallise for a moment—which is what happens when it thickens—and meanwhile brush over the top of the mould with some liquid soap. Make sure that the top of the gourd or fruit is still oily. If it is not, brush this with liquid soap too. The purpose of the soap film is to keep the two layers of plaster apart and to prevent plaster setting into plaster. Top up the mould box with plaster, making sure that there is a good thickness on top of the 'dome' of the fruit. Heap up extra plaster on top of this if you feel there is too small a space between the fruit and the surface of the plaster.

Leave to set as before. When you are quite sure that the plaster has set and dried, tip the plaster block out of the plastic box. It may be necessary to cut the sides of the plastic box with a craft knife to remove it. Now take a $2\frac{1}{2}$-inch wood chisel and insert it gently between the two halves of the mould. Lever the halves apart, being careful not to use too much force, otherwise you will break the mould. Take the fruit out of the mould, using a corkscrew to do this if finger pressure will not enable you to remove it. Examine the sides of the mould. If there are any cavities made by air bubbles, mix a very small amount of plaster and fill them in. Either brush the interior of the mould with liquid paraffin or submerge it for 4 hours in water to fill up the minute air pockets and prevent the wax sinking into the plaster. All you have to do to prepare the mould for casting is cut a small groove on both sides at the top and bottom of the fruit to hold a wick, a pouring hole into which you will pour the hot wax and an air hole to allow the air driven out by the hot wax to escape. Cut these hollows carefully in the plaster using a craft knife. The pouring and air holes are cut out as hollowed grooves, troughs which combine to make a circular channel once the two halves of the mould are pressed together. Both the pouring hole and the air hole should be cut at the top of the mould, that is on the side that will be uppermost when the wax is being poured in. They should both touch the fruit at the point where they will not spoil its shape and where they can leave a flash of wax which can be easily trimmed off. Fit a wick, stiffened with wax, down the axis of the mould with the ends on the two grooves and brush the interior surfaces of the mould with more liquid paraffin. Then fasten the two halves together with several stout elastic bands and tamp right round the edges of the join of the two halves with mould seal. This thick, tacky mastic is just as useful for sticking the two halves of improvised moulds together as it is for sealing round the top of a plastic or glass mould to prevent hot wax from pouring out of the wick hole. This precaution ought not to be necessary if you have cut good, deep, clean register marks, thus enabling the two halves to clamp together well, but it is better to err on the safe side than to have hot wax spurting all over the place.

Place the mould, pour-hole uppermost, on a sheet of newspaper. Make sure that it is sitting upright, and prop it up with blobs of Bostic Blue Tack if necessary to ensure that both pouring and air holes are in a vertical position.

Mix rather more wax than you estimate you will need. Heat a plastic funnel in hot water and put it in the pouring

FIG. 29 Plaster mould for a lemon candle

FIG. 30 The finished lemon candle

hole. Pour the wax at a temperature of 180°F (82°C) into the pouring hole until it comes out of the top of the mould.

It is difficult to break the well of the receding wax inside a mould of this sort, so to ensure that the surface of the candle fruit is properly moulded, follow the technique used by the wax fruit makers in Victorian times. Stop both holes with mould seal and shake the mould vigorously round in your hands as though you were working a cocktail shaker. The hot liquid wax should now be deposited on the outside of the candle and, when it cools, it ought to present an unbroken outer surface. Admittedly, the candle will be hollow in the middle but, as it burns, molten wax will pour into the hollow and fill it in. You can ensure that this happens by giving the candle a slightly smaller wick than it would usually have.

Leave the wax to cool overnight. Once you are sure that

it has cooled completely, delicately prise the two halves of the mould apart. To do this, insert a broad-bladed wood chisel into the crack between the two halves of the mould and lever them gently apart. Now is the moment when you will see whether you poured the wax at the right temperature. If it was too hot it may, in spite of the paraffin lining to the mould, have incorporated itself into the plaster.

A perfect wax fruit will probably emerge from the mould. However, despite the shaking up of the mould to ensure that the wax was forced into every nook and crevice, there may be some hollows caused by air bubbles. If so, melt a small amount of wax on the end of a palette knife over the flame of a spirit lamp and fill the hollow in.

It is more workmanlike, and certainly easier, to colour the fruit by adding an appropriate dye to the wax before it is poured. Once the fruit has been cast, wash it in case any small specks of plaster have adhered to the surface and then polish it with a very small amount of heated beeswax smeared onto a cotton rag or with a little aerosol furniture polish.

However, you may decide to paint the fruit for some reason. Perhaps the repair process with the palette knife has gone wrong, or you want a two-tone colour scheme for an apple which is green and red in patches. Do not use oil paints or the powder colours mixed with copal varnish which I recommend in Chapter 13 on candle painting. Use instead matt gouache paints or even coloured wax kept hot in an egg poacher.

Although fruit and gourds are the most obvious natural objects to imitate as candles, there are a wealth of others. Closed pine cones make good candle shapes, as do joints of bamboo, a twig and a few leaves, pieces of stag's horn, smooth pieces of driftwood, oddly shaped pebbles, shells and nuts.

These are just a few suggestions. Other possibilities you will discover for yourself.

12

The Decorated Candle

Decoration in a candle can arise as part of the candlemaking process or it can be added to a finished candle. An example of the first kind of decoration is a wick end tied in an ornamental knot—an experiment which, so far as I know, has not been tried out yet and which would make an improvement to the appearance of any candle, even if it did provide a few seconds' extra smoke.

The second kind of decoration should be added to a candle after it has been varnished. To varnish a candle, drive the point of an awl into its base where the bottom end of the wick is, and pick the candle up with the awl. You should avoid touching the candle with your fingers as far as is possible. Brush it over with a coat of clear-water spirit varnish in as few strokes as possible, working from the top to the bottom. Now drive a nail into the edge of a shelf and hang the candle up by means of a loop tied in the length of wick which I explained to you in Chapter 6 should be left protruding from the end of the candle for this purpose. Leave the candle to dry.

The decoration which you then add to your varnished candle could take the form of mica cut up into small pieces and stuck onto the shaft of the candle with blobs of wax glue so that they are positioned at angles to the flame at the top and reflect its light.

Gold leaf makes a royal display. Cut up pieces of transfer

gold leaf to exactly the size you require. You prepare the candle for this gold leaf by laying onto the varnished surface an adhesive known as 'Japan gold size', which will help the gold leaf to stick. Japan gold size can be bought from any art shop. You need not cover the whole candle with the size, just the parts where you want the gold leaf to stick. Now lift up the small cut-up pieces of gold leaf, still attached to the transfer paper, and lay them face down on the candle. Rub them down through the transfer paper. When you have laid enough pieces of gold leaf to make a pattern, hang the candle up to dry again by the loop in its wick. When the size has dried completely, remove the transfer paper from the gold leaf, peeling it off very gently. Then cover the candle with another coat of spirit varnish to enhance the gold and protect it until the candle is burned.

Letrafilm and Transeal are very thin coloured plastic sheeting used by designers and lay-out artists to design coloured work. These, too, can be applied to candles that have been varnished. The most elaborate colour schemes can be built up by the use of coloured film. This is semi-transparent and one colour can be overlaid by another.

First make a plan of the Letrafilm decoration you desire, then trace the shapes onto the back of a sheet of the coloured film. Cut round the shapes using a pair of embroidery scissors or a craft knife, such as the smallest size of Xacto knife. If you wish you can draw directly onto the coloured face of the Letraset, but to do this you must use a Radiograph pen of 0·1 thickness. Once you have cut out the shapes you want to apply, peel the backing sheet off them and stick them down on the candle's surface. They will adhere through their own tackiness. Varnish over them with spirit varnish, but never with any of the proprietary fixatives which may contain shellac.

Letraset lettering can be applied to candles in a variety of decorative schemes, although in my view it should always be used in colour or gold. I find black Letraset on a white candle very unappealing. Many simple ideas can be translated into real visual enjoyment by means of this adhesive lettering. How about a fat birthday candle with good wishes on it and perhaps a stave of 'Happy Birthday to You' with notes and words? A tall, thin candle could contain all the years of a person's life, down to his or her present birthday. A Christmas candle could bear seasonable greetings, and so on.

Decorations of all sorts can be pasted to the shaft of a varnished candle and can then be varnished over themselves to constitute a permanent appliqué. They can also be stuck down and overdipped in clear wax at a temperature of 210°F (82°C). These decorations can take many forms—stamps, small ferns slanting diagonally to the shaft of the candle, dried flowers and so on. The shorter the candle, the less likely is it to be extinguished by non-combustible debris of this sort collecting round the flame.

Grains of incense pressed into the shaft of a candle while it is still warm are an attractive and practical form of decoration. They will burn if they fall into the candle flame and will emit a perfume even if only slightly warm. They can also be arranged to form regular patterns or small pictures.

Some advanced techniques

The sand candle

If there is one form of candlemaking which has really achieved popularity in recent years it is the making of sand candles. The technique is not so very different from that used in casting natural objects. The principal difference is that the casting material is sand, not plaster. As you cannot have a double mould in sand, I am going to suggest that, instead of making the kind of sand candle which is usually seen nowadays, you create a part sand-cast, part plaster-cast candle. This will mean you do not have to stick to candles with flat tops, and it will also give your candles a touch of originality.

Begin by procuring a plastic box of the kind used for packing soft fruit. Half fill it with dampened fine sand. Now gently press down into the sand whatever you want to use for the model of the candle. An egg, or any kind of globular object, makes a good model.

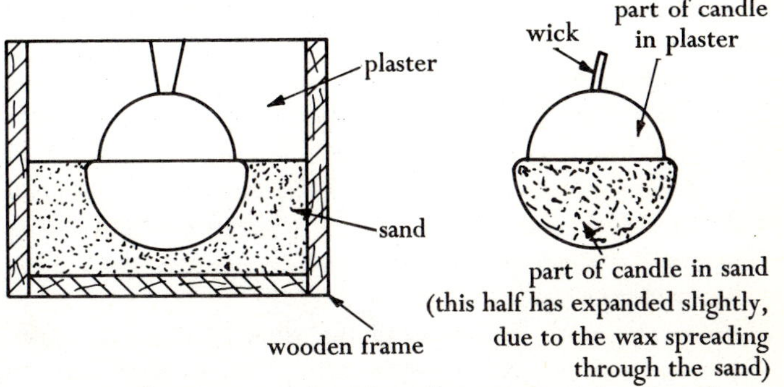

FIG. 31 Making an acorn-shaped candle, using a part sand- and part plaster-cast mould

While your model is still resting pressed halfway into the sand, pour plaster of Paris gently on top of it, as you did for casting in natural objects. Leave the plaster to dry hard, then gently remove it and set it aside. Drill a hole in the top of the plaster cast wide enough to allow hot wax to be poured in and air to escape. Carefully remove the model from its sand bed and flick away any grains of sand which have rolled into the bottom of the impression as these would mar the clean look of the candle once it had been cast. Cut a small block of solid paraffin wax, bore a hole in the middle of the block and place in the hole a pre-stiffened wick which has been dipped in hot wax several times so that it stands upright. The wick should just reach the brim of the hole through which the hot wax will be poured. The purpose of the block of paraffin wax is to break the force of the hot molten wax as it pours through the hole. If it were poured straight onto the sand, it might dig holes in it.

Instead of coating the plaster mould with liquid paraffin or liquid soap in the manner I have described previously in the book, try a different technique to prevent the hot wax from incorporating itself with the plaster. Immerse the plaster top of the mould in hot water for 10 minutes. Remove it and dry it very carefully by pressing it with a dry cotton cloth, forcing the folds of the cloth into the hollows of the mould without wiping it.

Position the plaster part of the mould on top of the sand half and run a little mould sealer round between the edge of the plaster and the side of the plastic box. Check that the wick is in the right position, then slowly pour in the wax until it has risen to the level of the top of the wick. Wait until a well forms and top up with more hot wax. The plaster mould can now be removed. It will have effectively moulded the top half of the candle. The lower half is still embedded in the sand. It can be lifted out and the sand dusted away. The hot wax will have sunk into the sand for some distance round the impress of the model. You will have to cut protruding parts of the sand away from the candle and perhaps run over the sanded bottom half with the flame of a methylated spirits or butane blow lamp until the bottom has assumed a smooth, symmetrical appearance.

Further projects can be carried out with the sand candle, such as cutting windows in the bottom half or positioning small shells, pieces of driftwood, fronds of seaweed or other ornaments on the top half to give the suggestion of a beach candle. As the sand candle burns down it will form a hollow, because the sand part will not fully melt owing to the fact that sand round the wax prevents it from attaining a sufficiently high temperature. It can then be used again by simply putting in a new wick and topping up with wax.

The water candle

From very early times people have been fascinated by the shapes which melted wax assumes when it is poured into water. A whole school of divination developed in Roman times whose followers pretended to predict the future by interpreting the meanings of the fantastic shapes that wax assumes when it cools quickly.

You can capitalise on the weird yet beautiful forms of rapidly cooled wax—forms which seem now like icebergs, now like clouds—by turning them into water candles.

Several different ways of making water candles have been evolved. The most direct is to position a substantial water bath, such as a plastic bucket half filled with water (look out for the overflow!), on your work bench and pour into it wax at normal moulding heat. The higher the distance from which you pour the wax and the more there is of it, the deeper the pinnacle it will form in the water. Try to pour a pinnacle for the centre first, following up with more wax poured gently in a semicircle round the pinnacle. Candles made in this way have to be wicked after they have cooled.

In order to wick them, drill a hole through the centre of the candle, either with a bradawl or with a stout piece of wire held in the chuck of an electric drill. A pre-stiffened wick which has been dipped several times in hot wax can now be inserted and sealed in by pouring a little melted wax between the wax and the wick.

To create an instant water candle, take a ready-made candle

of the required height (a wax taper will do) and anchor the tip of it to the bottom of the cooling bath with wax glue so that it stands upright and protrudes by a distance of an inch from the water. Now melt some wax and pour it on and round the base of the candle core which is sticking up out of the water. The wax will form an amalgam of fantastic shapes like the pinnacles and towers of some wind-sculptured desert mesa.

When the wax has cooled, remove the candle from the water and check to make sure that the surround has properly adhered to the candle core. If it has not, stick it in place with wax glue, or melt the core and the surround together by playing a blow torch gently upon both.

Both the water and sand candle can be quickly dyed in a variety of bright colours which will mix and merge by chopping up some small pieces of differently coloured dye disc and placing them on top of the candle. These are then heated with the blow torch until they melt and run down over the candle.

13

Candle Painting

The paints usually employed for candles are powder colour mixed with liquid soap, or metallic finishes applied by means of Goldfinger. On embossed candles these paints and finishes are often partially rubbed off so that the raised surfaces show as coloured wax and only the level parts are painted or gilded. This gives the candle what is known as an 'antique finish', suggesting that the paint or gilding has worn away through old age and usage.

Although powder and soap paint, and rub-on gilts are ideal for decorating many moulded candles—and are certainly the best media for children to use—for finer work it is necessary to turn to the traditional methods of candle painting developed by the Church craftsmen of the Middle Ages whose task it was to paint the great Paschal and other special candles used in abbeys and cathedrals. It is not surprising that the huge Paschal candle, which offered so much space for decoration, came to be ornamented by pictures and writing. At the head of the candle was a representation of the Crucifixion, with the extremities of the cross marked with grains of incense. Below was inscribed a table of all the important events that had ensued since the first Easter.

Against the white background of the refined beeswax from which many church candles were made, the paintings and inscriptions must have shown up like illuminated writing and miniatures on vellum. White wax makes a good background for any kind of painted decoration, and a plain rather than a sculpted surface provides a better medium. I shall therefore assume that for our first painted candle we will make use of a cylindrical or square candle, cast in the usual proportions of paraffin wax and stearin.

Decide which parts of the candle are to be painted. Traditionally only a band in the middle of the candle was painted rather than the whole candle. Mark out on a sheet of paper the exact area of the candle which is to be painted and draw out the design for the decoration on it. Now varnish the candle following the method described in Chapter 12 (p. 102). When the varnish is dry, cover the candle with a coating of egg white, thinned with a little warm water. Then hang the candle up to dry again.

Take the design for the painted decoration which you have prepared and lay it on a sheet of cardboard. With the point of the awl, prick through the lines of your drawing so that it is outlined in prick marks. Wrap the design round the candle, making sure that it is the right way up, and fasten it with a small piece of adhesive tape. Pick up some powdered colour on a cotton rag and rub it into the design through the prick marks, so that the outline of the design is printed on the candle shaft. Remove the cardboard and check whether any part of the design has failed to show up on the candle.

Lay the head of the candle on a 'candle pillow'. This is a linen bag, 6 inches wide, which is filled with clean, dry sawdust; it can be sewn from old handkerchiefs. Its purpose is to prevent the candle from moving about while it is being painted. A latex sponge, however, can be substituted for it.

Place a hand rest, which you can make for yourself out of three pieces of wood, over the base of the candle. This will prevent your hand from touching and smearing the design while painting is going on.

FIG. 32 A painted candle

Mix up some powder colours with oil copal varnish. I always buy my powder colours loose by the ounce in a colourman's (art materials supplier's). As they are stored in glass jars I can see exactly what colours I am getting. Mix each colour separately with the point of a palette knife in a china paint dish. Some artists prefer to mix their colours on a piece of plate glass, but it is handier to carry them about if they are in separate dishes.

Before you paint on the colours, do the gilding if you have decided to use gold in the design. As this is to be an artistically decorated candle, I suggest that you use real gold in the form of transfer gold leaf. Apply it in the way I have described in Chapter 12 (p. 102). When you have finished, carefully whisk away any pieces of gold leaf that have overlapped your design, using a soft brush so as not to spoil the gilding inside the design.

When the gilding has been completed to your satisfaction it is time to apply the colour. Paint the colours in with a long-hair sable brush. Leave them to dry. Colours mixed with copal varnish will dry on a candle fairly quickly, so it is a good idea to have two candles on the stocks, one which is in the process of being gilded and one which, having already been gilded, can be painted while the gold size on the other is drying. For some reason oil colours will stay wet on a candle almost indefinitely. Never use a fixative spray on a candle; most fixatives contain shellac which can be noxious if inhaled while burning. Burning copal has no such bad effects—in fact, copal incense was regularly burned before the gods in Ancient Maya.

When the painting process has been completed and all the colours have dried, wash the candle down with a soft sponge dipped in slightly warm water. This will remove the egg white, and with it any gold leaf which is sticking to parts of the design that have not been sized. Finally, apply a coat of mastic varnish over the whole design, again using a broad varnish brush and working from top to bottom. Hang the candle up by the loop in its wick and leave it to dry.

You will probably not want to set your beautiful painted candle alight straight away. Godfrey Leland, the ecclesiastical candle painter who was the recipient of traditional candle painting methods and from whom I have derived most of the information given in this chapter, had an ingenious suggestion to make on this score. He said that you could both have your cake and eat it by making a small engraved or ornamental shield and brazing to the back of it a collar or tube of metal to fit round the top of the painted candle. The bottom half of the collar would rest on the top of the candle; the upper half, however, would contain the base of another, shorter, candle which could be set alight so as to give the impression that the painted candle was burning.

Such a collar and shield sawn from thin sheet silver, soldered together and enamelled would have a very good effect. However, unless you happen to be skilled in silversmithing and enamelling, you would have to have some of the work carried out by someone else. I suggest that as a simpler alternative you make a tight-fitting wooden collar, with a cupped recess to catch wax drips, use it to fit the two candles together in the way that Leland describes and then paint it in the style of your candle. Cup rings of this sort occur on many candles of the past, such as the flambeaux carried by genii in Etruscan tomb paintings.

The designs for a painted candle can be either simple or complex. Obviously if you have in mind a Paschal candle or some other kind of religious candle you will employ some religious device—particularly the Paschal Lamb. Simpler lay designs could take the form of initials, foliage, birds or sprigs of flowers.

14

Candles for All Occasions

Outdoor candles

Generally speaking, ordinary indoor candles can be used out of doors, particularly if provided with a glass shade. The tendency of all candles, however, to go out or flicker a great deal when exposed to air currents can make it difficult and tiresome to sit at a barbecue by the light of indoor candles. Why not guard against this by making a large candle and coating the wick with an inflammable substance? For example, dip the wick in liquid wax and then in a heap of resin. This mixture of wax and resin will make the candle splutter a little but will increase its burning power. Alternatively, pickle the wick in a strong solution of boracic acid or saltpetre. But do avoid creating something that splutters so much that it is more like a firework than a candle.

An outdoor occasion such as a barbecue or a party is an ideal time to burn natural candles. The best known of these is possibly a reed which skewers a number of pieces of coconut or other oily nuts or berries (acacia berries might serve as experimental candles of the same sort). The oil from the coconut burns in the reed wick, but so too does the other material in the nut, producing a rather smoky flame which renders this type of candle unsuitable for anything but outside use. The small dried fish once used in Cornwall for candles would also burn well when threaded through with a wick. So too would Tung nuts, if they were obtainable. Any nut with a hollow or fairly spongy interior can be turned into a candle by drilling it, filling it with oil (preferably a sweet oil, i.e. almond or olive oil) and pushing a wick into the cavity.

The natural candle that has the oldest history here in Britain is the rush dip, a candle made by dipping the dried pith of a reed in wax. At the end of the eighteenth century the naturalist Gilbert White of Selborne sent the following account to Daines Barrington of how these candles were made in his parish: 'The proper species of rush for this purpose seems to be the *Juncus conglomeratus* or common soft rush, which is to be found in most moist pastures, by the sides of streams and under hedges. These rushes are in best condition in the height of summer, but may be gathered, so as to serve the purpose well, quite on to autumn. It would be needless to add that the largest and longest are best. Decayed labourers, women and children make it their business to procure and prepare them. As soon as they are cut they must be flung into water and kept there; for otherwise they will dry and shrink and the peel will not run. At first a person would find it no easy matter to divest a rush of its peel or rind, so as to leave one regular, narrow, even rib from top to bottom that may support the pith; but this, like other feats, soon becomes familiar even to children; and we have seen an old woman, stone blind, performing this business with great dispatch, and seldom failing to strip them with the nicest regularity. When these *junci* are thus far prepared, they must lie out on the grass to be bleached, and take the dew for some nights and afterwards be dried in the sun.

'Some address is required in dipping these rushes in the scalding fat or grease; but this knack also is to be obtained by practice. The careful wife of an industrious Hampshire labourer obtains all her fat for nothing; for she saves the scummings of her bacon-pot for this use; and if the grease abounds with salt, she causes the salt to precipitate to the bottom, by setting the scummings in a warm oven. Where hogs are not much in use, and especially by the sea side, the coarser animal oils will come very cheap. A pound of common grease may be procured for four pence; and about six pounds of grease will dip a pound of rushes, and one pound of rushes may be bought for one shilling, so that a pound of rushes, medicated and ready for use, will cost three shillings. If men that keep bees will mix a little wax with the grease, it will give it a consistency, and render it more cleanly and make the rushes burn longer . . . A good rush, which measured in length two feet four inches and a half, being minuted, burnt only three minutes short of an hour, and a rush of greater length has been known to burn one hour and a quarter.'

White does not tell his correspondent something which he probably knew already: that the rush dip was not burned in a candlestick, for it could not stand upright, but in a special holder, rather like a clothes peg on a stand, which gripped the dip and in which it was adjusted from time to time as it burned away.

In spite of the technique of rush-dip making followed by the cottagers of Selborne, it is not necessary to leave a thin strip of the outer husk on the reed before it is dipped. Nor is it necessary to subject it to quite such an elaborate process of bleaching and drying. I found it was enough to pull the outer covering off carefully a strip at a time, hang the rush pith up to dry and then dip it in hot wax. I began by using what was left in the frying pan, just as White recommends, but I feel that wax is more suitable. One reason for this belief is that the pith can be dyed bright colours either right along the stem or in bars of different colours at intervals and then dipped in clear paraffin wax without stearin. This will show up the colours to the best advantage. To colour the dips, simply brush them with a paint brush dipped in powder dye mixed with water. This is better than using poster colour, which might clog the flame of the dip too much. Fig. 33 shows the sort of simple wooden holder which could be made very easily for standing on a supper table at a barbecue or picnic after dark. Dips do not give quite as much light as candles, so use several of them in one holder.

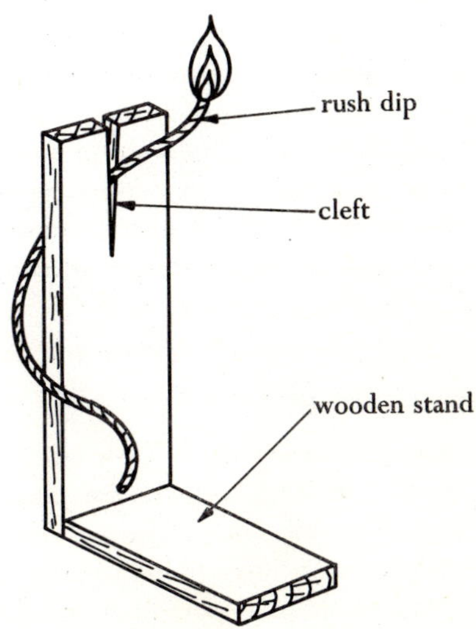

FIG. 33 A wooden holder for a rush dip candle

Candles for children

I said in the introduction that some of the best customers for candles nowadays are children—or rather their parents, who like to burn nightlights in their children's bedrooms. Any candle can be made to burn in a bowl of water while floating upright if you drive a large enough nail into its base to weight and balance it.

Children's candles not only capitalise on humanity's love of a naked flame (largely unfulfilled nowadays save for the candle). They can also explore nursery story characters like Humpty Dumpty. What a revenge on the wicked wolf in the tale of Red Riding Hood to set fire to him and watch him burn slowly away!

As well as providing delight at the recognition of familiar heroes, heroines and animals, candles can be made to work simple toys (always under parental supervision, please!). The easiest of these is a twisting serpent. It can be cut from stiff aluminium foil, such as the kind used to provide cases for pre-packaged foods, and painted in realistic colours in Humbrol enamels. It should be hung from a wire gallows just high enough over the candle flame to ensure that it turns well but does not burn.

Candlemaking for profit

Many candlemakers now market their wares in art and craft shops and by mail order. The new craft magazines which are currently springing up in some numbers form an ideal medium for advertising home-made candles. However, there is still nothing to beat a foot inside the door of an appropriate shop together with a compelling explanation of just why the shop-keeper should stock one's wares.

Very little has been done to provide souvenir candles depicting scenes from beauty spots or seaside resorts, or folklore characters associated with a particular area, such as the Lincoln Imp. Yet a candle is the only souvenir of which nobody need ever grow tired. It can always be lit and burned away.

Little has also been done by craft candlemakers to provide personalised candles for those who might be prepared to commission them—wedding candles, engagement candles, candles in school colours to celebrate scholastic success, etc. Emerson said that if you could only invent a mousetrap which was better than anyone else's, the world would beat a path to your door. It is equally true that, if you can design candles quite different from those made by other craftsmen, people will want to buy them.

I have not intended to imply that there is a royal road to making money from candles or that, if there is, I know it. However, there are several ways in which candlemakers could make more of themselves and their wares than they do. The candlemaker is a true craftsman and as such is much too modest about his achievements. I have just read a book by a very talented American lady about how to make money out of candlemaking. She is a professional candlemaker but nevertheless failed to impart her address to her readers on the jacket copy, the back of the jacket or even at the end of the preface which she wrote. Modesty of this sort can be self-destructive. After all, there are plenty of people who are just dying to buy the right kind of candles—your kind. So here are a few do's and don'ts for those who would like to sell their candles.

Have labels printed bearing your business address and attach them to every candle you sell. Submit entries to every exhibition for which you can hope to have an entry accepted, such as modern decor exhibitions. Wrap every candle in cellophane. This will help to combat dust, one of the great enemies of the good appearance of a candle. And try to sell to stores, particularly large furniture stores, instead of merely relying on your local craft shop.

15

Candelabra for Your Candles

Although it is as true now as it always was that 'men do not light a candle and put it under a bushel, but on a stand, and it gives light to all in the house', very few candlemakers give much thought to the type of candlestick that would set off their creations in the way they deserve. Much less do they deliberately set out to design and construct a candlestick that will suit the candle they are intending to mould. This is a pity, because a candle is a work of art in its own right. Like other works of art it should be enhanced and complemented by a setting of some kind. There are practical as well as aesthetic reasons why candles require stands, just as pictures need frames and statues pedestals. Although a candle may look very attractive burning away standing on its own base, it is not a good idea to allow it to do so. Unless the candle is placed in some sort of container there is always a possible fire risk, and there is certain to be a lot of spattered candlegrease which someone will have to clear up—provided, of course, that the grease does not become permanently embedded in the carpets and furniture before it can be cleared up.

Why should candlemakers be so indifferent to stands? One reason may be that the suppliers of craft materials for candlemakers make no attempt to induce them to use stands. It is very rare to see either in a shop or in a mail-order catalogue anything that will hold a candle. I can only think of one example—the special heat-resistant balloon glasses intended for perfumed candles. Rarely can you buy candlemaking equipment and candlesticks under the same roof, yet the candle and its stand ought always to be considered together.

A good candlestick should either complement the shape and colour of the candle it holds or act as a vivid contrast to it. It should raise the candle up, even if only a little way, so that its proportions can be considered as a whole and its light-giving qualities enhanced. It should try to cope with the problem of candlegrease by providing either a cup or a basin to catch the spilled wax, or at least a base onto which the wax will trickle and settle rather than falling on the floor.

Certain other qualities may or may not be desirable in a stand. Candlesticks that reflect light always seem to me to be particularly attractive; this is why I am fond of silver candlesticks. Candle holders of earlier times, for example the pricket candlesticks which spiked onto the bottom of candles, could accommodate candles of almost any size. This is a practicable idea if it can be achieved without sacrificing other considerations. It is perfectly easy to add a spike to any of the candlesticks discussed below, and equally simple to make a hole in the bottom of a candle so it will sit on top of the holder.

Perhaps the most important consideration when buying candlesticks is that they should be inexpensive. Candlemakers will want to spend any extra money they have available on buying more wax and accessories. Therefore in this chapter I shall confine myself to the kinds of candle holder that can be bought or constructed cheaply.

Antique candlesticks have a great charm, and they are not all ruinously expensive. They are, however, designed to accommodate commercially produced candles, which are usually several sizes smaller than those made by amateurs. An exception to this rule is the stand intended to hold the ceremonial candle made for religious use. Church candelabra were being made until quite recently, and you may be able to secure a reasonably modern example which would provide the qualities of good design and good workmanship that every candlemaker is looking for.

Old candlesticks and candelabra do not, generally speaking, command enormous prices, especially if bought from junk shops and scrap merchants. Old candle holders of the standing kind—bedroom candlesticks, wall bracket candle holders and hanging chandeliers—are all worth looking out for and buying if the price is right.

Antique candlesticks can be adapted quite easily. First decide what size of candle you intend to use in them. Hunt around for any metal container of just that size. It can be an aluminium jar of the kind used by chemists to store tablets, a tin of the sort used to pack silver polish, or simply an old tin can. Anything will do, provided that it is the right size. Cut off a section of the end of your chosen container, ½ inch deep, and paint the outside in bronze, brass or metal Humbrol enamel colours, depending on the metal of the antique candlestick. If for some reason you cannot find a ready-made metal cup of the size you require, then make one by cutting off a section of aluminium tube and filling in the bottom of the cylinder you have thus obtained with a disc of thin aluminium sheet, cemented with epoxy resin. Select a round wooden dowel the size of the diameter of the socket of your antique holder, glue it to the base of the metal cup and, when the glue has set, cement the cup into the candle socket.

In your hunt for antique candle holders you may well come across a real prize which you feel ought to be left intact because of its value as a work of art. Or you may purchase the kind of candlestick that does not pose any spill problems, such as the Victorian bedroom candlestick in which the candlestick proper rises from a flat tray, to which is attached a handle. In cases such as these, adapt the candle to the holder, rather than the other way round, by cutting off a short section of commercial sized candle and attaching it to the bottom of your home-made candle with wax glue.

There is a more direct way of obtaining antique candle stands, and that is to buy not old candlesticks but old containers with a diameter wide enough to admit home-made candles of the normal size. The range of small antiques that can be coaxed into holding candles is enormous. Often they can be purchased cheaply because they are chipped and broken; however, they are perfectly adequate for their purpose after a little repair work because the viewer's attention is diverted to the candle and any imperfections in the holder will pass unseen.

Just a few of the antiques that make ideal holders for large craft candles are: porcelain vases; earthenware and stone pots of the kind used to package mustard, pickles, preserves and honey; and all sorts of glass jars. A variety of objects, discarded and useless now, can take on a new lease of life if adapted as candle holders. Victorian flower holders and ink wells made from decorative stone, like serpentine, are a good example. Liquid measures, pewter pots, earthenware umbrella stands and many more objects which you can find for yourself will convert into splendid candle holders.

The contemporary candle holder designed in glass or china for craft size candles is usually very attractive but rarely cheap. You can make a custom-built wooden, stone or composite candlestick for a fraction of the cost of the shop-bought article, and your candlestick can be as modern as you like.

There is nothing difficult about candlestick construction. You have already mastered the first step by converting an antique candlestick. Once again, make up a metal cup from a tin of suitable dimensions. Do not bother to paint this cup, though; just sink it flush inside the top of the candlestick. To cut a hole for the cup in the candlestick, use a commercial hole cutter working in an electric drill, afterwards cutting up to the edge of the hole with a craft knife or wood chisel. If you are making a holder for a larger size of candle, use wood gouges of different sizes to excavate a big enough recess to hold the tin cup.

It saves much time if you can find a ready-made shape for a candlestick without having to carve it out from start to finish. Make a visit to a junk shop or breaker's yard to look for the turned wood finials that entered into much of the furniture of past generations: the ends of curtain poles, stair posts, bedstead knobs and so forth. The finial will probably be vase-shaped and have one rounded end, which would have been on show, and one flat end, where it joined a square wooden beam. Stand it up both ways to decide how it will look best.

Examine the wood of the finial. It may be made from mahogany or some other attractive hard wood. If it is, remove the varnish with paint stripper and a scraper, and then fill the grain of the wood with wood seal. You can darken the colour of the wood if you wish by rubbing it with linseed oil. Finish off by rubbing it with a good wax polish.

If your carved or turned wooden ornament is made from painted or varnished soft wood, strip it down. Repair any dents, damaged patches or cracks with Polyfilla, rub down with sandpaper, apply two coats of primer, rubbing down between coats, and finish with several coats of polyurethane high gloss paint. Choose a deep colour to reflect the light of the candle like the colours used in Chinese porcelain or lacquer.

Half or whole coconuts make excellent candleholders. If you intend to use a whole one, cut a hole with a hole cutter in the top, pour out the milk and scrape out the lining with a piece of bent wire. Sand down the nut to give it a wood seal finish, or french polish it before fitting a tin cup into the top to hold the candle. Half coconuts can be glued together by their apexes. A hole is cut through the bottom of the top half into the lower half with a hole cutter and a tin cup is sunk in so that it is flush with the bottom. Needless to say, coconuts should be polished inside as well as outside if they are used in halves in this way.

It is not difficult to make candlesticks from soft stone. If you own a lathe, you can turn stone into symmetrical shapes. Even if you possess a wood saw, some files, chisels and sandpapers, you can still produce attractive candle holders from such stones as alabaster, serpentine and Kimmeridge shale. As Kimmeridge shale will burn, it is wise to fit candlesticks made from this material with a tin cup.

Soapstone is another easy material from which to make candlesticks. It can be purchased from rock shops. This stone can be sawn very easily, filed and even carved with a penknife. It takes an attractive though not a high polish when rubbed with an abrasive mixed with oil. The other stones I have mentioned can also be treated in this way, although in the case of alabaster and serpentine the abrasive must be mixed with water, not oil. Saw the candle holder into its rough shape with a wood saw or hacksaw and remove any surplus material with files or rasps. Carve the stone with chisels, craft knives or penknives, and finish by rubbing down with coarse, medium and finally fine sandpaper. Now it is time to apply powdered abrasives, first a fairly coarse one, such as emery paper, followed by a milder one, like crocus powder.

A further medium for experimenting in making candle holders is modelling clay. There are several proprietary brands of modelling clay which once modelled set hard without needing to be fired. They can easily be made up into sculptured figures, at the top of which a stump of candle can be embedded to provide a cup of sufficient size to act as a candle socket.

Appendix

Candlemakers' Suppliers

Candlemaking is such a fast-growing hobby that suppliers to the craft are constantly increasing in number. I shall therefore not apologise to any of the candle craft suppliers whom I am bound to omit.

Candle Makers Supplies, 4 Beaconsfield Terrace Road, London W14 0PP, are one of Britain's largest suppliers of candlemaking equipment. They have a very wide range of materials, moulds and accessories, which they will supply both by mail order and across the counter. I have always found them very helpful with encouragement and advice, and they produce an extensive price list with all sorts of items not to be found in other suppliers' catalogues.

The Candles Shop, 89 Parkway, London NW1, is another supply firm with which I have dealt very happily in the past. It too provides a price list and order form, from which mail-order purchases can be made, as well as offering over-the-counter service.

Quite a number of complete candle kits are on the market. Candlemakers outside London who do not want to buy by mail order can purchase Reeves' complete candlemaking kit from the large number of Reeves stores scattered up and down Britain. Many art shops, craft shops and boutiques now stock at least some of the materials for candlemaking. If your local craft supplier does not, suggest to him that he is a little backward in this respect and that this is a line of hobby material which he just ought to carry on his shelves.

Anyone who wants to use unrefined beeswax may well have to buy it from a sculptor's shop, such as Tiranti, 72 Charlotte Street, London W1P 2AJ, rather than a candlemaker's supplier. Sculptor's shops also supply blocks of paraffin wax.

Cornelissens, 22 Great Queen Street, London WC2, will supply colours and gold leaf, together with the tools with which it is applied.

I should now like to refer the reader to some other candle equipment supply firms with whom I have not dealt myself but who have been recommended by other writers on the craft:

Allcraft, 61B High Street, Watford, Herts.
Cowling and Wilcox Ltd, 26–8 Broadwick Street, London
Hobby Horse Ltd, 15–17 Langton Street, London SW10.

TEACH YOURSELF BOOKS

PAPERCRAFT

Carson Ritchie

The art of papercraft can be as simple or as difficult as you want it to be. The materials are cheap, readily available and easy to use. This book provides the beginner with all the information he or she needs to embark on this varied and highly decorative art.

Every form of papercraft is covered in this book, ranging from paper toys, silhouettes and papercuts to collages, stamp pictures and rolled paperwork. Full and clear instructions are given throughout, along with designs for projects and ideas for further work.

A complete guide to papercraft, by a life-long exponent of the art, which both instructs and inspires.

ISBN 0 340 19817 6

UNITED KINGDOM	£1.25
AUSTRALIA	$3.95*
NEW ZEALAND	$3.95
CANADA	$4.95

*recommended but not obligatory

TEACH YOURSELF BOOKS

JEWELLERY MAKING

Del Fairfield

Jewellery making has often been considered inaccessible to the hobbyist. But this comprehensive and lucid introduction to the subject shows how the beginner, with the right equipment and the necessary technical know-how, can soon acquire the expertise to produce well-made and beautiful jewellery.

The author begins with the basics of jewellery making – tools and equipment, terms and techniques, materials – and progresses to the design and construction of a piece, and the different types of textures and finishes with which it can be decorated. Rings, cufflinks, chains, pendants, necklaces and earrings are among the pieces covered. Finally, the author includes a useful list of jewellery material supply houses throughout the country.

ISBN 0 340 20386 2

UNITED KINGDOM	**£1.50**
AUSTRALIA	**$4.90***
NEW ZEALAND	**$4.90**
CANADA	**$4.95**

*recommended but not obligatory

TEACH YOURSELF BOOKS

CREATIVE CRAFTS

Frederick Oughton

This book has been designed as a bank of ideas about craft methods and materials, to start the reader thinking, looking, perceiving and *doing* using only cheap or free materials.

The contents cover a wide field of craft materials and techniques, including paper, plaster, wood and clay, modelling, moulding, carving and design. The emphasis throughout is on explaining the basics of each craft, on starting points for the beginner and on finding fun and self-expression in craftwork.

Packed with ideas, advice and information, this book will provide just the stimulus needed by anyone who wants to get started in creative crafts but doesn't quite know where to begin.

ISBN 0 340 20379 X

UNITED KINGDOM	**£1.25**
AUSTRALIA	**$3.95***
NEW ZEALAND	**$3.95**
CANADA	**$4.95**

*recommended but not obligatory